FAST FORWARD 3

FAST FORWARD 3

Classbook

Marion Geddes

Oxford University Press

Oxford University Press, Walton Street, Oxford OX2 6DP
Oxford
New York Toronto Melbourne Auckland
Petaling Jaya Singapore Hong Kong Tokyo
Delhi Bombay Madras Calcutta Karachi
Nairobi Dar es Salaam Cape Town

and associated companies in
Beirut Berlin Ibadan Nicosia

Oxford is a trade mark of Oxford University Press

ISBN 0 19 432308 0

First Published 1986
Second impression 1987

Set in ITC Garamond by VAP (Group) Ltd
Kidlington, Oxford

Printed in Hong Kong

Several of the texts and exercises in this book were originally chosen and compiled for the Regent Schools' publication *General English Modules (GEMS)*. The author and publishers are therefore grateful to Rachel Belgrave of the Regent Schools and to the Regent Schools teachers or former teachers listed below for their contribution to this book. The *GEMS* from which material was taken are as follows:

Daily Life, compiled by Colin Campbell (the reading texts on pages 7, 8, 13, 16, 45, the exercises on page 13, the listening text on page 23, and the role-play on page 48); *Money*, compiled by David Barnes (the reading text on page 25 and the role-play on pages 28–9); *Communication at Work*, compiled by Sue Mornington (the reading texts on pages 58–61 and the role-play on pages 68–9); *The Media*, compiled by Karen Lewis (the reading text on pages 74–6); and *The Arts and Society*, compiled by Anthony Fagin (the reading text on pages 89–90, the exercises on page 91, and the role-play on pages 93–95).

Contents

Introduction
Thinking about language learning

This book offers you texts, exercises and activities to help you improve your reading and listening comprehension, to give you opportunities to speak English, and to help you expand your vocabulary. (Grammar exercises and writing activities are included in the Student's Resource Book.)

Before you start, you will find it useful to spend a little time thinking about the three language skills that this book focuses on – reading, listening and speaking – and about ways of learning vocabulary.

Reading

1 Reading texts

Make a list of all the things you have read, in any language, in the last two days. Don't forget to list things like:

notices
advertisements
street maps
a telephone directory
labels on medicine bottles

How many of the things were written in English? Compare your list with other students.

2 Reasons for reading

Why did you read each text? Make a list of your reasons.

3 Ways of reading

How did your reasons for reading influence the way in which you read each text?
Did you read quickly or slowly?
Did you read silently or aloud?
Did you read from the top to the bottom of the text, or did you jump around?

4 Reading in English

Perhaps most of your reading in the last two days has been in your mother tongue. Do you need, or do you want to read, the same kinds of text in English?

Flick through this book. What kinds of reading material does it include?

Listening

In discussing reading, you have talked about:

variety of reading texts
reasons for reading
ways of reading

What are some of the similarities between listening and reading? What are some of the differences?

Speaking

Do you agree or disagree with these statements? Discuss them with other students.

'I don't speak very much because I'm afraid of making mistakes.'

'I always try to say what I want to say – even if it means I make a lot of mistakes.'

'I want to be corrected all the time.'

'I don't like to be corrected when I'm speaking.'

'I want to speak only with the teacher. I'll learn "bad" English from the other students.'

'I find it useful to practise speaking in pairs and groups.'

Vocabulary

1 Learning new vocabulary

The word 'flick' on the previous page may have been new to you. How did you find out its meaning? Did you:

guess it?
look it up in a dictionary?
ask your neighbour?
ask the teacher?

If you flick through this book again and say 'flick' several times aloud, do you think it will help you remember the word and its meaning? Why/Why not?

Is 'flick' a word that you want to remember? Why?/Why not?

2 Recording new vocabulary

What techniques do you use to record new vocabulary? Do you write it down:

in a special vocabulary book?
in a multi-purpose notebook?
on cards?
in alphabetical order or as it occurs in the lesson?
with a variety of coloured pens?

What techniques do you use to record its meaning? Do you:

write down a translation in your mother tongue?
write down an English explanation?
use drawings or diagrams to illustrate its meaning?
use any other techniques?

3 Reviewing new vocabulary

What techniques do you use to review new vocabulary? Do you review it:

aloud or silently?
while listening to some music?
on the bus going home?
last thing at night?
any other way?

Are there any techniques that other students use that you would like to try?

The Plural Problem

1

Write the singular of these words:

1 boxes	5 feet
2 oxen	6 teeth
3 geese	7 these
4 mice	8 brethren

2

As you read the poem, listen to it on the cassette.

Why English is so hard

We'll begin with a box, and the plural is boxes;
But the plural of ox should be oxen, not oxes.
Then one fowl is goose, but two are called geese;
Yet the plural of moose should never be meese.
You may find a lone mouse or a whole lot of mice.
But the plural of house is houses not hice.
If the plural of man is always called men,
Why shouldn't the plural of pan be called pen?
The cow in the plural may be cows or kine,
But the plural of vow is vows not vine.
And I speak of a foot, and you show me your feet,
But I give you a boot – would a pair be called beet?
If one is a tooth and a whole set are teeth,
Why shouldn't the plural of booth be called beeth?
If the singular is this and the plural is these,
Should the plural of kiss be nicknamed kese?
Then one may be that, and three may be those,
Yet the plural of hat would never be hose.
We speak of a brother and also of brethren,
But though we say mother, we never say methren.
The masculine pronouns are he, his and him,
But imagine the feminine she, shis and shim!
So our English, I think you'll agree,
Is the trickiest language you ever did see.

Anon.

From *The Faber Book of Useful Verse*

3

Underline all the words in the poem which are *not* correct English.

Spelling and Pronunciation

1

How are the words in italics pronounced?

1 This meat is so *tough* I can't eat it.
2 The *boughs* of the apple tree are laden with fruit.
3 I've got a cold and a terrible *cough.*
4 Bread *dough* is made from flour, water and yeast.
5 The burglar came in *through* the window.
6 The poor baby has got an attack of *hiccoughs.*
7 I've got guests coming so I must give the house a *thorough* cleaning.

2

Now read the poem. As you read, listen to it on the cassette.

Of moths and mothers, coughs and boughs

I take it you already know
Of tough and bough and cough and dough?
Others may stumble, but not you
On hiccough, thorough, laugh and through.
Well done! And now you wish perhaps
To learn of these familiar traps?

Beware of heard, a dreadful word,
That looks like beard and sounds like bird.
And dead: it's said like bed not bead,
For goodness sake, don't call it deed!
Watch out for meat and great and threat,
Then rhyme with suite and straight and debt.

A moth is not a moth in mother
Nor both in bother, broth in brother,
And here is not a match for there,
Nor dear and fear for bear and pear.
And then there's does and rose and lose –
Just look them up: and goose and choose,

And cork and front and word and ward
And font and front and word and sword.
And do and go and thwart and cart –
Come, come, I've hardly made a start!
A dreadful language? Man alive,
I'd mastered it when I was five!

Anon.

From *The Faber Book of Useful Verse*

3

. . . . and to finish off:

There once was a writer named Wright
Who instructed his son to write right;
He said, 'Son, write Wright right.
It is not right to write
Wright as "rite" – try to write Wright right.'

Anon.

From *1000 Jokes for Kids of All Ages* (Ward Lock)

What word was the boy trying to write?

Read the rhyme aloud, paying particular attention to stress.

1 Eat, drink and relax

You are invited . . .

Look at the invitations. Which party would you prefer to go to? Why? Think of three or four reasons.

In pairs, find out which party your partner would prefer to go to and why.

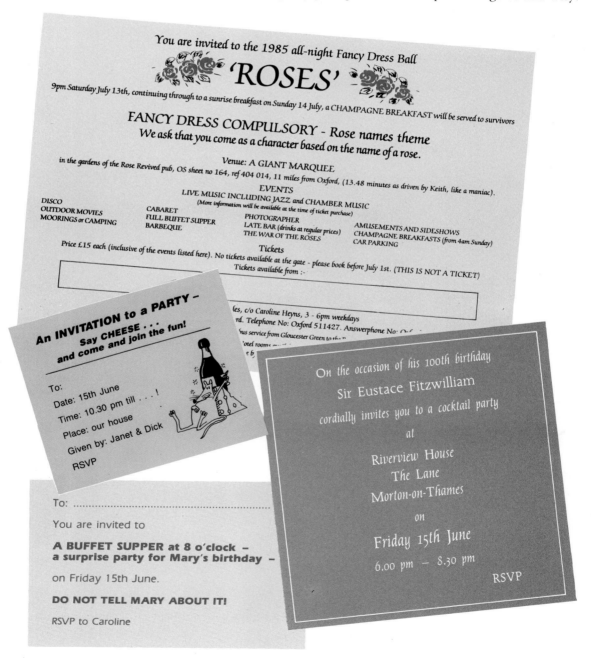

You are invited to the 1985 all-night Fancy Dress Ball

'ROSES'

9pm Saturday July 13th, continuing through to a sunrise breakfast on Sunday 14 July, a CHAMPAGNE BREAKFAST will be served to survivors

FANCY DRESS COMPULSORY - Rose names theme
We ask that you come as a character based on the name of a rose.

Venue: A GIANT MARQUEE

in the gardens of the Rose Revived pub, OS sheet no 164, ref 404 014, 11 miles from Oxford, (13.48 minutes as driven by Keith, like a maniac).

EVENTS

LIVE MUSIC INCLUDING JAZZ and CHAMBER MUSIC
(More information will be available at the time of ticket purchase)

DISCO
OUTDOOR MOVIES
MOORINGS or CAMPING
CABARET
FULL BUFFET SUPPER
BARBEQUE
PHOTOGRAPHER
LATE BAR (drinks at regular prices)
THE WAR OF THE ROSES
AMUSEMENTS AND SIDESHOWS
CHAMPAGNE BREAKFASTS (from 4am Sunday)
CAR PARKING

Tickets

Price £15 each (inclusive of the events listed here). No tickets available at the gate - please book before July 1st. (THIS IS NOT A TICKET)

Tickets available from :-

...les, c/o Caroline Heyns, 3 - 6pm weekdays
...rd. Telephone No: Oxford 511427. Answerphone No: ...
...bus service from Gloucester Green to the ...
...otel rooms ...

An INVITATION to a PARTY –
Say CHEESE . . .
and come and join the fun!

To:
Date: 15th June
Time: 10.30 pm till . . . !
Place: our house
Given by: Janet & Dick
RSVP

On the occasion of his 100th birthday
Sir Eustace Fitzwilliam
cordially invites you to a cocktail party
at
Riverview House
The Lane
Morton-on-Thames
on
Friday 15th June
6.00 pm – 8.30 pm
RSVP

To: ....

You are invited to

A BUFFET SUPPER at 8 o'clock – a surprise party for Mary's birthday –

on Friday 15th June.

DO NOT TELL MARY ABOUT IT!

RSVP to Caroline

Party Food

1 Imagine you are planning an informal party with some drinks and snacks. Some food and drinks stimulate the nervous system and make people talk more than usual – just what you want for the party to go well. Look at the lists below and put a tick beside ten items of food and drink that you think are good stimulants. Compare your choices with a partner.

Food	**Drinks**
strong cheese	Coca-Cola
processed cheese	orange juice
mild cheese	coffee
grapes	tea
salted peanuts	white wine
potato crisps	red wine
pickled herrings	champagne
chicken liver pâté	tequila
French bread	sangria
cucumber sandwiches	Chianti
hard-boiled eggs	
peppermint chocolate	
fruit cake	
sausages	

2 Now read the article *Talk and Cheese.* As you read put a cross in the lists above beside the items of food and drink that the author thinks are most appropriate for a lively, happy party. How do *your* choices compare with the author's?

Note: These instructions give you a *reason* for reading the article. What is the reason? How do you think it will affect the *way* you read the article? (e.g. Will you need to understand every word?)

Talk and Cheese

food to put you in party mood

Throwing a party? Well, make it a cheese and wine do, if you want it to go with a swing. There's nothing to beat them for getting people talking.

Mature Cheddar, Brie, blue cheese and Stilton are good choices. They have something processed cheese spreads don't have – tyramine, a stimulant to the central nervous system.

Tyramine has similar powers to amphetamine, which is known to make those who take it talkative.

You can't go far wrong with wine either. But remember that white wines are greater stimulants than red wines (with the notable exception of Chianti) and are never more effective than when served with strong cheese.

If you want to offer red wine, go for a wine with some stimulant properties of its own, such as Chianti and sangria.

Or have a good champagne. During the fermentation process, that talk-inducer tyramine is formed. This is possibly why champagne is used in celebrations and why it has the reputation of being a truth serum.

Of all the spirits, tequila seems to be the most stimulating.

The reason is not clear. One explanation is that tequila is often served in a cocktail called a Margarita, with salt on the rim of the glass. The salt is an old tradition but it serves a chemical function as a mild anti-depressant.

Using it can result in a 'happier' drink and less of a post-drink crash.

This salt effect might also explain why some people insist on putting salt in their beer and why salted peanuts and crisps are popular with alcohol.

Strangely, pickled herrings help to loosen tongues, and so do chicken livers.

Herbs and spices enliven both food and conversation, mainly by delighting the palate and the sense of smell. Saffron, peppermint, nutmeg and pepper are especially effective.

The talk food of our time is coffee – the most popular drink in the world.

It contains the stimulant caffeine, and Brazilian coffee has more than any other.

The original Coca-Cola was perhaps one of the most effective social drinks.

During the late 1800s and early 1900s, its combination of cocaine, alkaloids of the kola nut (predominantly caffeine), other flavourings and sugar made it a chemically powerful brew.

Cocaine has long been outlawed and most cola drinks these days have artificially added caffeine. However, Coca-Cola is still made from coca leaves – without the cocaine.

From the *Daily Mirror*

3 Often one can *guess* the meaning of a word or phrase from its context. You may not always be able to guess the exact meaning. However, the *general* meaning may be sufficient to enable you to understand the whole text.

Without looking at the original text, write down as many alternative words and phrases as you can to fill in the gaps below.

TALK AND CHEESE

Food to put you in party ____1____

____2____ a party? Well, make it a cheese and wine ____3____, if you want it to ______4______

There's nothing ____5____ for getting people talking.

Now look back at the text and find what words and phrases the writer uses.

4 Find these phrases in the article and *guess* what they mean.

1 a post-drink crash (l 36)
2 to loosen tongues (l 42)
3 by delighting the palate (l 44)
4 a powerful brew (l 58)
5 outlawed (l 59)

Relaxation and Inspiration

1 This article discusses aids to relaxation and inspiration. Before you read it, discuss relaxation and inspiration aids (food, drink, yoga etc.) that you find useful and that help you work and think creatively. Make a list of aids.

2 Read the text and underline all the relaxation and inspiration aids mentioned. Would you be willing to use all of them?

Think with a drink

ALCOHOL is well known to relax the inhibitions. It helps people to ''let go'' and can set the stage for originality and inspiration.

William Faulkner said he couldn't begin writing without a bottle of Scotch nearby, and many other writers have used alcohol to fire their creative urge.

Ernest Hemingway was one. Only he needed coffee and cigarettes, too, and eventually contracted lung cancer, probably caused by his heavy smoking.

Drink is one of four basic types of aids to inspiration. The other three are:

- Stimulants such as coffee, tea and chocolate.
- Drugs that alter the state of consciousness, such as mescaline and LSD.
- Mixed stimulant-depressants, such as red wines and cigarettes.

Large meals seem to act against creative impulses. Perhaps the old cliche that an artist has to be hungry to reproduce his best work has basis in fact as well as finances.

Fasting, on the other hand, seems to induce an altered state of mind. Religions throughout the world recognise this and almost all of them include some fasting as part of their ceremonies.

The key to LEARNING seems to be plenty of protein.

But avoid depressants such as beer – it contains hops which are a sedative – jasmine tea, thyme and marijuana.

From the *Daily Mirror*

3 One way to help you remember the meaning of new words is to *write* them in ways that illustrate their meaning. This is how two students used this technique to remember the meaning of *mood* and *to throw a party*.

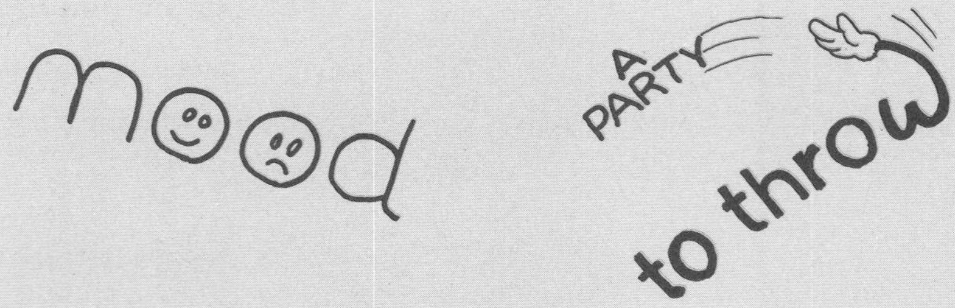

Choose three or four words or phrases either from the two articles or that have come up in your discussions and that you want to remember. Write each one in a way that illustrates its meaning.

Walk around the class and look at how other students have written their words.

Food Proverbs

1 Match the two halves of each proverb correctly.

Half a loaf is . . .	*. . . over spilt milk*
The proof of the pudding is . . .	*. . . the broth*
Too many cooks spoil . . .	*. . . in one basket*
One man's meat is another man's . . .	*. . . better than none*
You can't have your cake . . .	*. . . in the eating*
Don't put all your eggs . . .	*. . . poison*
It's no use crying . . .	*. . . and eat it*

2 Explain the meaning of each proverb.

Advice through Rhymes

1 **A hangover cure**

Last evening you were drinking deep
So now your head aches. Go to sleep;
Take some boiled cabbage when you wake;
And there's an end of your headache.

Alexis (c.350 BC)

What advice would *you* give to a friend suffering from a hangover?

2 Vegetables and fruit for health . . .

An apple a day
Keeps the doctor away.

If you an iron tonic need
Eat more spinach, beet and swede.
If your nerves are all awry
Lettuces and onions try.

What aspect of your health are carrots supposed to be good for?
Can you think of other vegetables or fruit and their benefits?

3 Eating peas . . .

I eat my peas with honey,
I've done it all my life.
They do taste kind of funny,
But it keeps them on the knife.

. . . and celery

Celery raw
Develops the jaw.
But celery, stewed,
Is more quickly chewed.
Ogden Nash

. . . with tomato ketchup

If you do not shake the bottle,
None'll come, and then a lot'll.

From *The Faber Book of Useful Verse*

Tongue Twisters

Practise saying these tongue twisters as *quickly* and *accurately* as possible.

1 *The big baker bakes black bread.*

2 *The bun is better buttered, Bill muttered.*

3 *Cheryl's cheap chip shop sells cheap chips.*

4 *A rhinoceros rushed into a restaurant and ordered ribs of beef, rabbit, rolls, raspberries, radishes, rhubarb pie and rice.*

5 *You can have:*
fried fresh fish
fish fried fresh
fresh fried fish
fresh fish fried
or fish fresh fried

6 *All I want is a proper cup of coffee*
Made in a proper copper coffee pot.
You can believe it or not –
I want a cup of coffee
In a proper coffee pot.

Tin coffee pots or
Iron coffee pots,
They're no use to me.
If I can't have a
Proper cup of coffee
In a proper copper coffee pot
I'll have a cup of tea.

From *An Anthology of British Tongue Twisters* by Ken Parkin (Samuel French)

English Vines and Wines

How many of these statements do you think are true?

1 The vine has been cultivated in England since Roman times.
2 Today there are about 230 vineyards in Britain.
3 Over the last ten years the area devoted to viticulture has increased dramatically and shows no sign of stopping.
4 High-quality English wines have won prizes in several important wine competitions.

Many people will be surprised to know that all the statements on page 11 are true. Connoisseurs think well of English wine. They find it elegant, fruity and often well made, if a bit expensive.

The unreliable English climate makes the present revival of vine cultivation difficult to explain. What may at first have been regarded as a hobby is now being seriously considered as a commercial enterprise. Farmers are reported to be digging up fruit trees in order to plant vines. Businesses are being sold to finance the planting of vineyards.

Some vineyards in England are fully commercial, for example Lamberhurst Priory in Kent with its 33 acres (13.4 hectares). At the other end of the scale are vineyards like Frithsden, a small 2½ acre (1 hectare) vineyard near Hemel Hempstead, north of London. For its owner, Mr Latchford, vine growing is still a pastime. However, by now he is able to break even and cover his costs. The 5000 to 6000 bottles he produces annually are sold locally in and around Hemel Hempstead.

From *Business Express* (Modern English Publications)

1 On the cassette you can listen to an interview with Mr Latchford. *Before* you listen, *guess* the answers to these questions:

1 What made Mr Latchford and his wife start thinking about growing their own vines?
2 What did they do to find out more about vines and vine cultivation?
3 How many vines did they order from Germany to start their own vineyard?
4 How did they find a suitable site for their vineyard?
5 Who does the work in the vineyard?

2 Now listen to the interview. As you listen, find out how well you guessed the answers to the questions in Exercise 1, and answer these questions:

1 When is the grape harvest?
2 How many gallons of juice does Mr Latchford usually get? (Note: 1 gallon = 4.5 litres)
3 Which year has been the best so far?
4 What are the prospects for this year's harvest?
5 Does Mr Latchford believe his vineyard could eventually become a commercial proposition?

English Pubs

1 Use *not more than two minutes* to write down anything you know about pubs in Britain.

In groups, ask other students what they know about pubs and share what you know with them.

2 Look at the headline of the article below. What do you think the article is about?

Read the article. Are you surprised by any of the information it reports?

Good beer and good cheer top pubs list

by Nikki Knewstub

A national survey on the public's attitude to beer and pubs, has made the none-too-startling discovery that the pub is the most popular place of entertainment for most people.

The survey, conducted by Market and Opinon Research International, was made for the Brewers' Society and appears in the current edition of its quarterly magazine, *Brewing Review*.

It found that half the men in the UK and a quarter of the women, visit a pub at least once a week. About half the pub-goers have a local which they prefer to any other. Women are almost as likely as men to have a regular pub.

But the sexes diverge when it comes to what they want – apart from drink – from a pub. They agree that cleanliness, comfort and friendly bar staff are the most important criteria, but women put clean toilets top of the list in judging a pub. Men judge it by the friendliness of the bar staff, closely followed by whether it is used by their friends.

Third most important among the men is whether their favourite beer is on tap, whereas this hardly interests women at all. The fastidious female puts clean glasses after clean loos, closely followed by comfortable seats, then friendly bar staff.

Younger men claim to drink the most, but 55 per cent of beer drinkers say they drink no more than two pints per visit. Only 10 per cent of those questioned wanted a reduction in the age limit of 18 for drinkers, and 11 per cent wanted it raised.

Most men (88 per cent) normally drink beer, but 67 per cent of women drink other types of alcohol, particularly spirits. Men under 24 prefer draught lager, but draught bitter still holds its own as the overall favourite tipple.

From the *Guardian*

3 In groups, discuss what questions the researchers must have asked in their interviews. Write down the questions.

If you are studying English in the UK:

1 Report back to the rest of the class and agree on a set of interview questions.
2 Prepare a questionnaire using these questions.
3 Use the questionnaire to make your own interviews, for example with other students; your landlady/landlord; people in pubs.
4 How do your findings compare with the findings reported in the article?

If you are studying English outside the UK:

1 In groups, devise similar questions about pubs, bars or restaurants in your country.
2 Prepare a questionnaire using these questions.
3 Use the questionnaire to interview other students in the class.
4 How do your findings compare with the findings reported in the article?

2 ▸▸ People

Find Someone Who . . .

Read through the sentences below and check that you understand them.

As you do this exercise walk around the class and talk to as many people as possible. When you *find someone who . . .*, write his/her name in the 'names' column below. Find as many *different* names as possible.

Find someone who . . .	Names
1 jogs or runs at least three times a week	....
2 has had a slipped disc or suffered from other back troubles	....
3 has seen sheep being clipped	....
4 knows what a 'Mars bar' is	....
5 collects stamps, coins or beermats	....
6 has been to Africa	....
7 sometimes wears purple	....
8 can tell a joke in English	....

The Lakeland Sheep Farmer

The map on the next page shows a small part of the Lake District in the north west of England. An area of great natural beauty, the Lake District is visited by thousands of tourists every year, in particular by hill walkers, campers and outdoor enthusiasts. The Lake District is also an important sheep-farming area. The sheep are a hardy breed who roam the hills during the summer months and in winter often have to suffer weeks of snow outdoors.

1 Visitors to the Lake District are made immediately aware of its dialect, not only by the speech of farmers and others born and brought up in the area, but also by place names and suffixes.

Look at the two lists of words. Find examples of the Lakeland words on the map and guess their meaning. Match each word with its Standard English equivalent. The first one has been done for you.

Lakeland words		**Standard English words**
1 dale	☐	a stream or river
2 beck	☐	a small lake
3 water	☐	a large lake
4 fell	☐	a mountain, hill or moor
5 crag	☐	a cliff
6 tarn	1	a valley

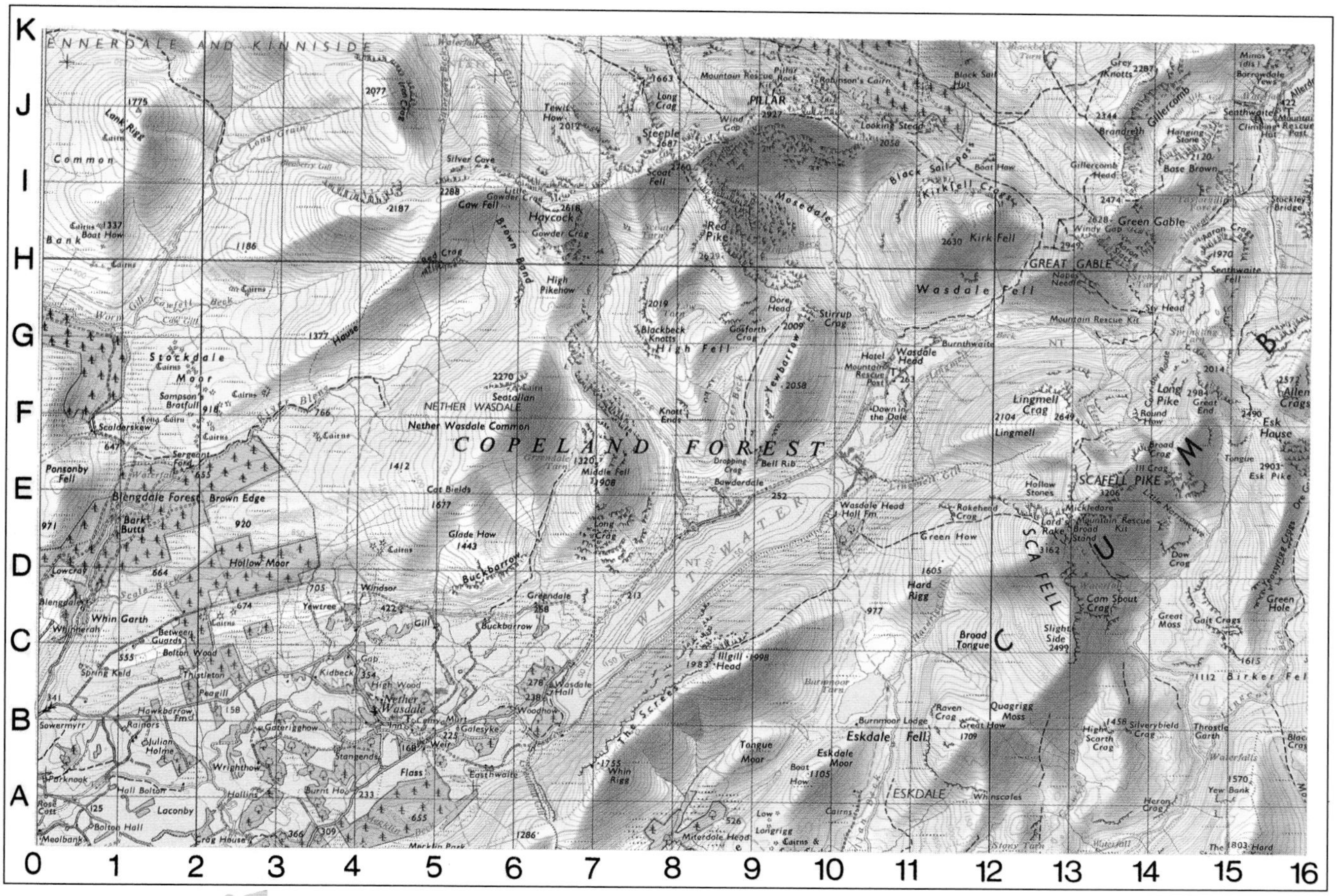

■ Lake District

2

Joss Naylor, a Lakeland sheep farmer, lives in Wasdale Head at the foot of Scafell. Find these places on the map.

Look at the photographs of Joss Naylor. What impression of him do you get from them? Discuss with your partner and make notes using these headings:

Personality
Working life
Spare time activities
Diet
Health

3 Now read the article. As you read, make notes using the same headings as in Exercise 2.

A LIFE IN THE DAY OF JOSS NAYLOR

“I usually wake about six and lie awake till dawn. I never sleep very well. I've been in pain since I was nine with disc trouble. I've had many operations, worn corsets, strait-jackets, the lot. The surgeons have told me many a time to give up farming and running. I was off 54 weeks with my back when I was 20. Some nights I get only a couple of hours sleep. The last three months have been about the best in my life.

I go down about seven and pour myself a mug of hot water from the kettle on the Aga. Then when the rest get up for breakfast I have some Weetabix* with a spoonful of Alpen.* I used to have egg and bacon till about four years ago. I just lost the taste for bacon, at least the bacon they sell today.

I wear an old pair of trousers and old pullover, the same ones practically every day, and me boots. In the summer I often work in shorts and vest and running shoes. I never shave in the morning. I might not shave at all, not for several days, unless I'm going out in the evening. The first job of the day is milk the cow. I do it by hand. She gives about three gallons which I put in the fridge to cool. We drink yesterday's for our cereal.

I never eat anything during the day. All I take with me is a Mars bar.** If I get hungry I might have a few mouthfuls of spring water on the fells. Hunger soon passes if you drink. I finish when it's too dark to work.

I lose around 50 sheep a year. Some die of starvation in the snow. Last year we had snow till June up here. They just waste away and a strong wind topples them over. Then maggots can get them, eat them alive; or foot rot, or foxes.

When I come down from the fells I have a scrub down in the beck. In the summer I get in up to my waist and give myself a good scrub. This time of the year I just take my boots and socks off and wash my legs, freshen up. Perhaps once a fortnight I might have a bath. Perhaps once a month.

I have a bit of cake and a drink of tea with the missus. The kids (Gillian 12, Susan 10, Paul 9) are usually home around this time. Then I go out again, just round the farm, do some sorting, or clipping, depending on the time of the year. I milk the cow again and then feed the dogs. They get milk straight from the cow, and their maize. We have our dinner about 6.30, bit of mutton, bit of beef, whatever the missus has got, then a cup of tea afterwards. I watch TV some nights. I like all sport. And I like a good comedian. Three or four nights a week I'm out giving a bit of a talk on fell running. Last night I was at the Wigton Round Table in Caldbeck.

When I have a race on, I have to try to get ahead with my work. You can't get anyone to look after sheep these days. Nobody's daft enough. There's no money in sheep farming. I'm lucky to end up with £2000 at the end of the year. For something like the Lakes 24-Hour Race I might be clipping almost all the night before.” (In 24 hours he did 72 peaks of more than 2000 ft. – a world record.) “It's even more awkward when I have to travel away, like the Three Peaks Race – Snowdon, Ben Nevis and Scafell” (which he did in 11 hours, 54 minutes) “or the Welsh Peaks” (14 peaks of 3000 ft. in 4 hours 46 minutes).

I never ran as a lad. My back was too bad. I didn't do my first race till I was 24. It was a Mountain Trial, here at Wasdale Head. I hadn't entered. I just joined in when they set off, in my working boots. I was first to the first check point, joint first to the second, then I fell down with cramp in both legs. I came in last in lots of races, passing out with the pain at the barrier. It wasn't till I was 31 that I was any good. I'm now 41 and I don't think now I'll get any better. I like being fit and I love the Lakeland scenery. I love the sunsets, the solitude. It's like Paradise up there.

I usually finish the day with a drink of coffee and a piece of the missus's cake. I never read books. We don't get a paper out here, just the *News of the World* on a Sunday. We're in bed by about 11.30. I wear nowt in bed. The missus will play war for telling you that. If a fella's fit, he doesn't feel the cold. And if a fella's fit he can work to make himself warm.”

Hunter Davies

**well-known brands of breakfast cereal*
***a chocolate and toffee bar*

From *The Sunday Times*

4 Look back at the notes you made in Exercise 2. How does the impression you have now of Joss Naylor compare with your first impression?

Are there facts which you learned while reading about his life that surprised you? In pairs compare any surprises you had.

5 The author of the article chose to call it A LIFE IN THE DAY OF . A more ordinary title would have been A DAY IN THE LIFE OF . . What is the author trying to convey in the title?

6 The article is written as a transcript of Joss Naylor's speech. A more usual style would have been to report the words, something like this:

> Joss Naylor's is not an easy life. A poor sleeper, he is awake by six and up at dawn. He has been bothered by disc trouble from the age of nine and . . .

Which style do you prefer? Why?

7 As you read the article you may have noticed some examples of Lakeland dialect. Look back at the text. How many can you find? What are their Standard English equivalents?

8 Choose a partner and find out how he/she spends a typical day.

9 Describe situations in which you might:

give up eating sweets and cakes
use a mug instead of a cup
give yourself a good scrub
want to freshen up
lose the taste for some particular foods
try to get ahead with your work
suffer from cramp
set off from home earlier than usual to get to work

10 In line 35 Joss uses the word *mouthful*. Do you know any other expressions with the pattern *noun + ful*?

The Baobab Tree Collector

Born in the United States, Ellen Drake has spent most of her working life in Africa working in wild-life conservation and tourism. She is also a writer and is at present engaged in research for a book on the baobab, a tree that is found in many parts of the African continent.

1 Read the text and look at the photographs. What is unusual about baobab trees, compared to other trees? What kind of climate do you think they grow in?

> Perhaps two thousand years old, some baobabs are now thought to be amongst the oldest living plants. They doubtless have achieved this great age through close adaption to their environment. Their huge swollen grey boles, often as much as ten feet thick, are so soft that a rifle bullet can travel through them. They are semisucculent, contain a woody tissue, but no hard wood, and they are also protected by a thick, glossy, grey bark, smooth in texture and effective in preventing water loss.

From *Africa, A Natural History* by Leslie Brown (Hamish Hamilton)

The fruit of the baobab

A baobab in Senegal

A baobab in Botswana

A baobab in the Malagasy Republic

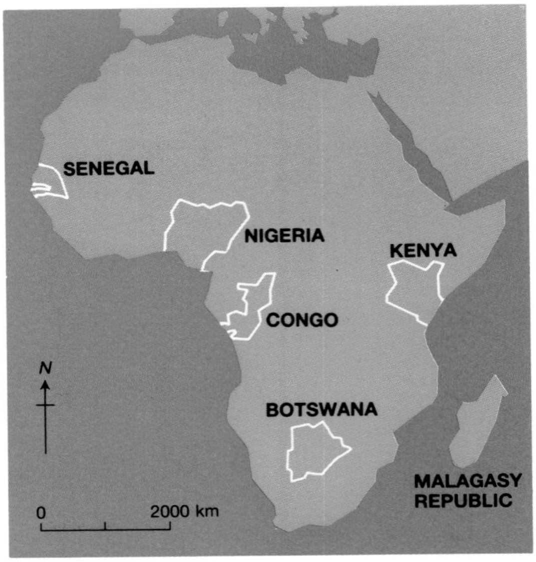

2 On the cassette you can hear an interview with Ellen Drake. Listen to the interview and answer these questions:

1 Why did Ellen decide to write about baobab trees?
2 What words does she use to describe baobab trees?
3 Why is the baobab tree called 'the upside-down tree'?
4 What can the baobab tree be used for?

3 What kind of things do you think will be in Ellen's book? Who do you think the readership will be?

What Word am I Thinking of?

This is a game for reviewing vocabulary. It can be played in small groups or with the whole class. All books should be closed.

Take it in turns to think of a new word or phrase you have learned in this unit, and that you want to remember. Explain the meaning of the word or illustrate it on the blackboard, but do not say what the word is. The other students must guess what the word or phrase is.

Student A: I'm thinking of an adjective that is used to describe a plant that stores water.
Student B: Succulent.

Warning

1

Listen to the poem on the cassette without looking at the text. Then listen and read.

Warning

When I am an old woman I shall wear purple
With a red hat which doesn't go, and doesn't suit me,
And I shall spend my pension on brandy and summer gloves
And satin sandals, and say we've no money for butter.
I shall sit down on the pavement when I'm tired
And gobble up samples in shops and press alarm bells
And run my stick along the public railings
And make up for the sobriety of my youth.
I shall go out in my slippers in the rain
And pick the flowers in other people's gardens
And learn to spit.

You can wear terrible shirts and grow more fat
And eat three pounds of sausages at a go
Or only bread and pickle for a week
And hoard pens and pencils and beermats and things in boxes.

But now we must have clothes that keep us dry
And pay our rent and not swear in the street
And set a good example for the children.
We will have friends to dinner and read the papers.

But maybe I ought to practise a little now?
So people who know me are not too shocked and surprised
When suddenly I am old and start to wear purple.

Jenny Joseph

From *Rose in the Afternoon* (J. M. Dent)

2

Answer these questions:

1 About how old is the woman in the poem?
2 What does she believe is the advantage of old age? Do you think she is right?
3 What examples of middle-aged respectability are given in the poem?

3

When and why do people feel the need to conform?

How would you like to behave when you are old?

Medical Jokes

Many jokes depend on puns – the use of two words that sound the same, or of a word that has two meanings. Can you identify the puns in these jokes?

A little girl attending the school clinic started crying as the doctor approached her.
'I'm only going to take your pulse,' the doctor explained.
'But don't I need it?' sobbed the little girl.

A plump young woman went to see her doctor.
'I'm worried about losing my figure, doctor,' she said.
'You'll just have to diet,' said the doctor unsympathetically.
'What colour?' asked the woeful patient.

A patient whose doctor advised him to get away to the seaside for a rest and a change came back after a week and went to report to the doctor.
'Well, did the rest and change do you good?' asked the doctor.
'Not much,' said the disgruntled patient. 'The doorman got my change and the hotel got the rest.'

Patient: Doctor, doctor – I can't sleep! It's driving me crazy. I can't sleep I tell you!
Doctor: You should lie on the edge of the bed. You'll soon drop off.

From *1000 Jokes for Kids of All Ages* (Ward Lock)

Practise telling these jokes aloud using lots of expression. You don't have to use exactly the same words, providing of course you use the pun!

3 Holidays and travel

Amazing Facts and Figures

Information from *The Guinness Book of Records*

1. Divide into an even number of groups made up of three or four people. Half the groups (the As) will look at the information on this page. The other groups (the Bs) will look at the information on page 22. The As and Bs have different information.
2. Look at the information for your group. Together *guess* the missing facts and figures. Write your guesses in the table.
3. As and Bs should now join up in pairs. Find out from your partner the correct missing information. Compare it with your guesses. Score each of your guesses like this:

   a poor guess 0 a reasonable guess 3 an excellent guess 6
4. Compare the scores of each pair. Which pair is the winner?

Information for group A	Correct information	Your guess	Your score
1 The world's largest hotel			
Country:	USSR		
No. of rooms:	?	___	___
No. of lifts:	?		
No. of employees:	about 3000	___	___
2 The world's most expensive hotel accommodation — Country:	?		
Cost per day:	US$5500	___	___
3 The world's most expensive passports — Country:	?		
Price (in 1982):	about £172	___	___
4 Man who has visited most countries — Name:	Jesse Rosdail	___	___
Nationality:	?		
Profession:	Teacher	___	___
No. of countries visited:	?		
No. of miles/kms. covered:	1,626,605m (2,617,766km)	___	___
5 Tourists visiting UK in 1982 — Number:	11,637,000	___	___
Total amount spent (excluding fares):	?		
6 Fastest round-the-world trip on scheduled flights — Name:	David Springhall	___	___
Nationality:	British	___	___
Time taken:	?		
			Total score:

Information for group B	Correct information	Your guess	Your score
1 The world's largest hotel			
Country:	?	____	____
No. of rooms:	3200	____	____
No. of lifts:	93		
No. of employees:	?		
2 The world's most expensive hotel accommodation			
Country:	France	____	____
Cost per day:	?		
3 The world's most expensive passports			
Country:	USSR	____	____
Price (in 1982):	?		
4 Man who has visited most countries			
Name:	Jesse Rosdail	____	____
Nationality:	American (USA)	____	____
Profession:	?		
No. of countries visited:	219	____	____
No. of miles/kms. covered:	?		
5 Tourists visiting UK in 1982			
Number:	?		
Total amount spent (excluding fares):	£3,184,000	____	____
6 Fastest round-the-world trip on scheduled flights			
Name:	David Springhall	____	____
Nationality:	?		
Time taken:	44 hrs 6 mins	____	____
			Total Score:

A Narrow Escape from Death

Christine Anderson is an English nurse. Recently she spent a year in New Zealand working as a nurse. She returned to Britain overland, travelling through Asia and Europe for five months. While she was in Thailand she narrowly escaped death.

1 Imagine you are a newspaper reporter working for a small local newspaper. You have been asked to write a story in a weekly series 'Narrow Escapes from Death'. You have a few notes about the incident Christine was involved in but you are not sure if they are correct. Read the notes.

NARROW ESCAPE FROM DEATH
(Christine)

young man clubbed to death
y Thai youths. 1 of them
=English.
Christine Anderson spent
night on beach with these men.
Drugs (hash?) involved.
Reason for murder - probably
a quarrel while all were
stoned.

2

Christine has recorded on tape what happened. As you listen . . .

1 check that your notes are correct. Put a tick beside the items that are correct; put a cross beside the items that are incorrect.
2 make notes about what happened so that you can write a story about Christine's narrow escape from death.

3

Compare your notes with a partner. Listen again if necessary.

4

What impression do you have of Christine? Look at the list of adjectives and underline those that you think describe her well. Add others if you wish.

foolhardy	naive
adventurous	sensible
courageous	intrepid

5

Write a short newspaper story about Christine Anderson (circa 300 words) entitled 'A Narrow Escape from Death'.

Kenya Safari

Keith Jarvey is a freelance journalist. He and his wife Jennifer and her sister Marjorie are thinking of going together on a holiday in Kenya.

All three prefer a holiday that offers a bit of adventure, rather than sitting around in comfortable hotels at a beach resort.

They enjoy camping but Jennifer in particular hates all the chores like putting up tents, cooking on a camp fire, washing up, etc.

They don't like going around with a large group of tourists. Ten people is about the maximum.

Marjorie enjoys her privacy and would not like to have to share sleeping accommodation.

Although Keith doesn't mind simple accommodation he wants to be sure that the holiday accommodation will include a hot bath every night.

They are very interested in wildlife.

1 Read *quickly* through the description of the Kenya Safari holiday. In pairs, discuss whether the holiday would be suitable for all three of them.

KUONI Kenya Safari

A four-wheel-drive safari vehicle, a large tailormade two-man safari tent with verandah, an enthusiastic, experienced driver and crew of three to prepare your meals and erect the tents, add the rugged Kenyan terrain and a thorn tree silhouetted against the moon, then you have the real Safari!

If what you want is a hot bath and cocktails before dinner every night, then forget it – if you feel like leaving the world behind and seeing some of the best scenery and game in Kenya, then read on . . .

WHAT YOU NEED TO KNOW

1. The Safari is completely inclusive of everything except alcoholic drinks. Clients should arrange with the leader (during the Safari briefing) for the purchase in Nairobi of drinks required on Safari. Most clients spend less than £20 on safari (including drinks).

2. You need to bring tough safari clothes, good shoes, a hat for the sun and dust, a torch, a sweater for cold evenings, toilet kit and towels. Maximum 1 suitcase only please. (You can leave surplus luggage in Nairobi.)

3. Transport is by Land Cruiser safari vehicle with roof hatches, max. three vehicles per safari. The staff do the cooking, erect the tents, make the beds and wash the dishes.

4. Tents are mosquito-proof and for two persons (for smaller single tents the supplement is £35 per week) and include bedrolls, mattresses, camp chairs, gas lights. Meals are served from the mess tent and there is a separate toilet tent and shower tent erected on each campsite.

5. Discouraging notes for those who would **not** enjoy this safari:
No hot bath after a dusty day in the bush, here you get a bucket shower (warm!). Electric razors are out – it's a beard or brush and soap. No cocktail bar and après-Safari set . . . we sit round the fire with a mug of tea. And remember this Safari is an adventure not a pursuit of first-class hotels and haute cuisine, and it's hell when it rains!

2 The article below was written by Keith Jarvey on his return from Kenya. Read the headline. What impressions does it convey to you about the safari holiday?

Read the article. Was the holiday a success? Why/Why not?

A WARRIOR STOOD WATCHING US, HIS BLANKET WRAPPED ROUND HIM AND A COUPLE OF SEVEN-FOOT SPEARS IN HIS HAND

'Don't stray out of the camp too far,' said Pat Fitzgibbon who was leading the 16-day safari. 'A lion killed a cow in this area only yesterday.'

The warning was not necessary. After all, we had been safe in London only two nights before – and here we were camped above a remote tropical river, loud with the sound of bird song and cicadas. As we ate dinner cooked over a camp fire, we looked warily into the darkness beyond the flames.

Had we really paid £494 each (with £73 fuel surcharge on top) to Kuoni Travel in Dorking to get warnings of this kind? Perhaps World Wide Life, who had sponsored the holiday, had got it wrong and the animals were a menace after all.

My wife and I retreated glumly to our tent, which was cosy or claustrophobic according to our mood, and reflected that we had 1,200 miles of travel in the eight-ton truck ahead of us.

Next morning life was far better. The tent had remained up all night, though we had never put one up before, no one had even heard the lion, and bacon, eggs and baked beans – the standard breakfast each day – raised morale anyway.

We spent the day driving round the game park, and with the benches facing outwards, animals were easy to see. Coming on your first elephants or pride of lions is enormously exciting – even if you have told yourself, as I did, that they would be very like those in London Zoo. Creeping along in single file to observe the hippos snorting and grunting in the river, or getting up early to see giraffes coming down to water, is better still.

Dirt tracks took us north, but the truck was surprisingly comfortable and some people read books on the way. The country through which we passed varied from the highlands, like some neat, tropical Sussex, to the arid bleakness of the desert with its cacti, black volcanic rocks and jagged lunar mountains.

By the time we reached Lake Turkhana our tongues would be hanging out with the heat. That, at least, was the warning, but we arrived just as the skies opened for the first downpour in a year. Early November produces the short rains, which fall at night in the form of light showers, but seven years of drought, followed by a sodden 1978, showed that the rules had altered.

'Think of the perfect bank holiday in midsummer,' said the brochure, 'and that is what your holiday will be like.' As we lay underneath the truck sheltering from the thunderstorms eating slightly sandy sandwiches, it did bring back memories of many a rained-off August treat.

This time, though, a warrior stood watching us, his blanket wrapped round him and a couple of spears in his hand. His wife, beside him, had tiers of rings from her neck to her breasts and their three children danced joyously in the downpour.

They had not dressed up for the tourists any more than the dancers at the lake had done. They had seen the truck stop just off the road, which was an event, given that we had only seen one other vehicle on the road all day. And so they had come over.

Pat, our guide, not only smelled out lions as he drove, but was a source of endless erudition, on anything from the male weaver bird's habit of imprisoning his mate in a tree, to the reason why hippos eat on land and fan out their dung with their tails before returning to water.

Expenses were minimal. The tour provided everything but alcohol and beer was cheap to buy. The only other cost came on photographs. If you wanted to take pictures of people you paid for them. Negotiations started at five Kenyan shillings (30p), but the going rate is one or two.

But service generally was admirable. When we returned, tired and dusty, to Nairobi four hours before a midnight flight, we had expected a wash and mince and spaghetti. We were all provided with bath, Scotch and dinner in a city restaurant.

The only curse was the weather. But, guaranteed a similar trip well away from the rainy season, we would both depart immediately.

From *The Guardian*

3

Imagine you are Keith Jarvey. Complete the Kuoni questionnaire about your safari holiday.

In pairs, compare your completed questionnaires.

KUONI

Dear Kuoni Client

We sincerely hope that you had an enjoyable holiday and that the arrangements made on your behalf were satisfactory. If not, we have every reason to seek your comments about it.

We also hope that you will travel with us again, and to help us continually improve our arrangements, we should be most grateful if you would complete this Questionnaire, fold it, and post it back to us. Thank you.

1 Your name? K. JARVEY	*3 Which month?*
2 Where did you go? KENYA	*4 Which tour?* SAFARI

PLEASE ✓ AS APPROPRIATE			*ADDITIONAL COMMENTS YOU MAY WISH TO MAKE**
5 Was the accommodation satisfactory?	☐ *YES*	☐ *NO*	
6 Was the food satisfactory?	☐ *YES*	☐ *NO*	
7 Was the transport comfortable?	☐ *YES*	☐ *NO*	
8 Was the cost of the tour reasonable?	☐ *YES*	☐ *NO*	
9 How was the tour leader? ☐ *VERY SATISFACTORY* ☐ *SATISFACTORY* ☐ *UNSATISFACTORY*			
10 Did you feel you were taken 'off the beaten track'?	☐ *YES*	☐ *NO*	
11 Would you go on a similar tour again? ☐ *DEFINITELY YES* ☐ *PERHAPS* ☐ *DEFINITELY NOT*			

**Please use separate page for additional comments if necessary*

4

Where do you think Jarvey's article was originally published?

☐ in the 'Travel' section of a daily newspaper
☐ in a Kuoni advertising brochure
☐ in a scientific magazine about Africa

Give reasons for your choice.

5

Work in groups of five or six.

1 Think of a country that you have enjoyed visiting or would like to visit. Tell the others in the group your choice. If two or more students have thought of the same country, they should choose another country, so that the group finishes with a list of five or six countries.
2 Write down the names of the countries across the top of a page of your notebook and draw columns, each with a country as a heading.
3 Write each of the words below in any of the columns, according to the association you feel between the word and the country.
4 Explain some of your associations to the others in the group.

to stray	cosy	arid	a downpour
remote	claustrophobic	jagged	a curse
a menace	morale	lunar	a drought
glumly			

The idea for this exercise comes from *Vocabulary* (in the Oxford University Press series *Resource Books for Teachers*) by John Morgan and Mario Rinvolucri

6 travel, a journey, a trip, travels, a voyage

Complete these sentences by using one of the words from the list above.

1 The . . . . . to London and back takes about 4 hours.
2 I am going on a . . . . . to the States, combining business and pleasure.
3 My hobbies are . . . . . , music and tennis.
4 He has been to Africa, Asia and South America. He should write a book about his . . . . . .
5 . . . . . is only for the rich.
6 The . . . . . round Cape Horn took three weeks.
7 Bye! Have a good . . . . . !

7 Walking

How do you move when you . . .

creep in single file?
walk in a crocodile?
stroll through the park?
stride along the street?
crawl along the floor?
walk on tiptoe?
stagger out of the pub?
limp and have to use a stick?

8 Animals

1 Find two verbs in Keith Jarvey's article that describe noises made by hippopotamuses.
2 Find a noun in the article that describes a group of lions.
3 What noises do these animals make? Match the correct verbs with each animal.

Verbs

to grunt	to moo	to neigh	to purr
to miaow	to bark	to growl	to quack
to cluck	to roar	to croak	to baa

4 What words can be used to describe a group of . . .

sheep? ducks? cows? elephants? puppies or kittens?

Planning a Holiday in Kenya

Role-play

Roles: Tourist, Travel Agent.

Decide whether you would like to be a Tourist or a Travel Agent and read through your role card.

Role card: Tourist
You are thinking of going on holiday to Kenya with your husband/wife and two children (daughter 7 and son 13). You would like to go for two weeks in November. As this would be your first visit to Africa, you want to get as much information as possible from a travel agent before you finally decide whether to go or not. You don't mind whether you stay on the coast or go inland. All of you would like to see some wild life.

1 In a group with other Tourists, discuss the questions you would like to ask the Travel Agent about your proposed holiday. Then prepare a checklist for yourself using headings like: Clothes; Accommodation; Flight information etc. You will need at least 15 headings on your list.
2 Find a Travel Agent and use the headings on your checklist to ask questions. Make notes about the information the Travel Agent gives you.

Role card: Travel Agent
You are a Travel Agent specializing in package tours to East Africa.

1 Read the information about holidays in Kenya on page 29. If there are words or phrases you don't understand, use a dictionary or ask another Travel Agent.
2 Make notes, or underline information that you think is *particularly* useful for tourists making enquiries about holidays in Kenya.
3 In a group with other Travel Agents test that you are familiar with all the information. Ask each other questions, e.g. 'What's the weather like on the coast in April?'; 'Do tourists need visas?' etc.
4 A Tourist will visit you to get some information about holidays in Kenya. Give advice and make suggestions. Before the Tourist leaves you, give any information that is important but that the Tourist has not thought of asking you for.

Information for Travel Agents

Kenya

THE GOING RATES

Flight time: Weekly London-Mombasa charter night flights: 10 hours approx. including stop in Rome for pick-up passengers and re-fuelling. Advance clocks 3 hours to Mombasa time.

Temperature and Climate: Average coastal temperatures, 83-87°F; hot on inland plains; cooler in hills. Short rains (intermittent, unpredictable, short-lived) November. Long rains March-June. Best dry seasons: September/October, and December-March.

Package Holidays: In both cases below prices are based on two-week stays per person and include flights, transfer from Mombasa airport to accommodation, and half or full board as stated. Both Enterprise and Sovereign offer reduced prices for children 2-12 years. Enterprise offer limited "one child free" holidays (book early for this concession). Enterprise sample prices: Self-catering £298-£349 (apartment only), based on occupancy for four persons; Hotels (Malindi) £375-£439 (half board) according to season; Hotels (Kikambala Beach and Watamu) £372-£505 (full board). Sovereign sample prices: Self-catering from £350 each (5-6 persons sharing), from £420 each (3-4 persons sharing), apartment only; Hotels £295-£750 (full board) according to season and category

of hotel. While British Airways offer only the Kenya beach holidays with direct flights from Mombasa (brochures available from their own shops or local travel agents) they naturally have plenty of competition. Thomas Cook, Wings and Martlet, for example, also have big Kenya programmes, with flights via Nairobi.

Safaris and Excursions: United Touring Company: Mombasa city, 75sh; Tsavo Game Park, one day, 495sh; two days with overnight accommodation, 835sh. Tsavo East/West and Amboselli, three days with overnight accommodation, 1,750sh. Glass-bottomed boat trips to coral reef: average 400sh for boat and up to four passengers; additional passengers, about 50sh each.

Currency: 14.80-15.25 Kenya shillings to £1 sterling (variable); best rates are for traveller's cheques. No Kenyan money available in UK, and none must be taken out of Kenya. Cash

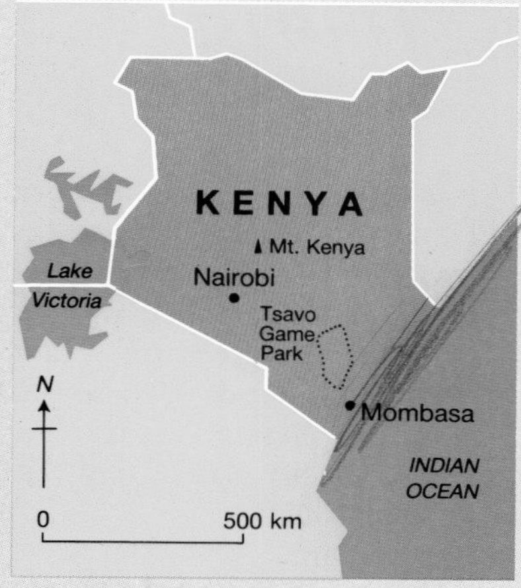

transaction forms for record of exchange and spending provided; keep safely as they are required on departure.

Souvenirs: Carved woodwork (ebony most expensive but good), basketwork, shells, gem stones, wall prints. Wide variety of plain and printed flimsy cotton wear (shirts, skirts, shorts, dresses, lengths of tie-round cottons).

Clothes: Swim suits vital; all else lightweight as possible; all very casual including evening wear. Sun glasses, sun tan cream and lotion, insect repellent; thin slacks/shorts in unobtrusive colours for safari; binoculars, camera.

Vaccinations: Advised: yellow fever, cholera, typhoid. Smallpox at present not required, but consult your doctor before going. Precautions against polio and malaria also advised.

Visa: Not required for UK visitors.

Information: Kenya Tourist Office, 13 New Burlington Street, London W1. Telephone: 01-839 4477.

Trials of a Tourist

1 Read and listen to the poem. Where would you normally read phrases like these?

TRIALS OF A TOURIST

It is three o'clock in the morning.
I am in a hurry.
I will have some fried fish.
It does not smell nice.
Bring some coffee now – and some wine.
Where is the toilet? There is a mistake in the bill.
You have charged me too much.
I have left my glasses, my watch and my ring, in
the toilet.
Bring them.

Porter, here is my luggage.
I have only a suitcase and a bag.
I shall take this myself.
Be very careful with that.
Look out! The lock is broken.
Don't forget that.
I have lost my keys.
Help me to close this.
How much do I owe you? I did not know I had
to pay.
Find me a non-smoking compartment, a corner
seat, facing the engine.
Put the case on the rack.
Someone has taken my seat.
Can you help me to open the window?
Where is the toilet?
I have left my ticket, my gloves and my glasses
in the toilet.
Can they be sent on?
Stop! I want to get off again. I have got into the
wrong train.

Who is speaking?
Wrong number!
I don't understand you.
Do you speak English?
I am an Englishwoman. Does no-one here speak
English?
Wait. I am looking for a phrase in my book.
My bag has been stolen.
That man is following me everywhere.
Go away. Leave me alone.
I shall call a policeman.

You are mistaken. I didn't do it.
It has nothing to do with me. I have done nothing.
Let me pass. I have paid you enough.
Where is the British Consulate?
Beware!

Bring me some cottonwool.
I think there is a mistake in your calculations.
I do not feel well.
Ring a doctor.

Can you give me something for diarrhoea?
I have a pain. Here.
I have pains all over.
I can't eat.
I do not sleep.
I think I have a temperature.
I have caught a cold.
I have been burnt by the sun.
My skin is smarting. Have you nothing to
soothe it?
My nose is bleeding.
I feel giddy.
I keep vomiting.
I have been stung by sea-urchins.
I have been bitten by a dog.
I think I have food-poisoning.
You are hurting me.
I shall stay in bed.
Bring me some brandy – please.
Help!
Fire!
Thief!

Anne Tibble

From the *Faber Book of Comic Verse*

2 In pairs choose three or four phrases from the poem. Imagine an incident when a tourist used them. Tell your story to the rest of the class.

4 ▸▸ The human brain

The Two Sides of the Brain

From *The Brain Book* by Peter Russell (Routledge and Kegan Paul)

The fact that the human brain is divided into a left and right half is not a new discovery. Once the skull is removed the division is obvious to the naked eye, and it is a common feature of brains throughout the animal kingdom. What is interesting about this division in man is that each half seems to have developed specialized functions, the left side appearing to do better at some tasks and the right side better at others.

1 Below is a list of some characteristics of the human brain. Match each characteristic with the appropriate explanation. The first one is done for you.

Characteristics of left and right hemispheres of the human brain	Explanations
1 verbal	☐ putting things together to form wholes
2 non-verbal	[1] using words to name, describe, define
3 spatial	☐ thinking in terms of linked ideas, one thought directly following another, often leading to a convergent conclusion
4 logical	☐ awareness of things, but minimal connection with words
5 linear	☐ drawing conclusions based on logic: one thing following another in logical order – for example a mathematical theorem or a well-stated argument
6 synthetic	☐ seeing where things are in relation to other things, and how parts go together to form a whole

Adapted from *Drawing on the Right Side of the Brain* by B. Edwards (Fontana/Collins)

2

On the cassette you will hear a talk called *The Two Sides of the Brain*.

You may already know something about this topic. In that case:

1 *Before you listen*, label the picture below using the six characteristics of the left and right hemispheres listed on the previous page.
2 Listen to the talk.
3 Compare how you have labelled the picture with what the speaker says about left and right hemisphere characteristics.

The topic may be new to you. In that case:

1 Listen to the talk.
2 Label the picture below using the six characteristics of the left and right hemispheres listed on the previous page.

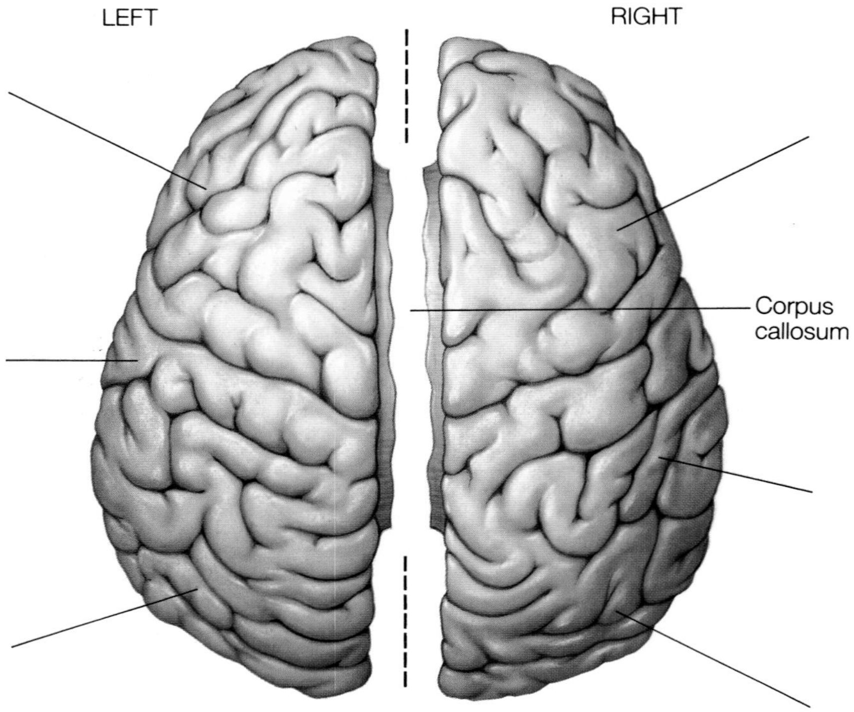

Now answer these questions:

1 What is the 'crossover effect'?
2 The speaker describes the results of two 'split-brain' experiments. What do the results indicate about left and right hemisphere characteristics?
3 The speaker believes we could improve the efficiency with which we use our brain in two ways. What are they?

3

Look back at page 8 (Exercise 3). Which right hemisphere function are you using when you try to remember a new word by writing it in a way that illustrates its meaning?

4

Can you remember any of the pictures that were used in Unit 1 to illustrate food proverbs? Look at page 9; why do you think pictures are included on this page?

5 Match each idiom with the correct explanation.

1 to rack one's brain about something
2 to pick someone's brains
3 to have something on the brain
4 to have a brain-wave

☐ to have a good thought or idea which comes unexpectedly or suddenly

☐ to think repeatedly or constantly about something

☐ to think very hard or for a long time to try to find a solution to a problem

☐ to talk to someone about a problem to get to know and later use his knowledge or ideas on that matter

Explanations from *English Idioms and How to Use them* (Oxford University Press)

Now use the appropriate grammatical forms of the four idioms to replace the pictures.

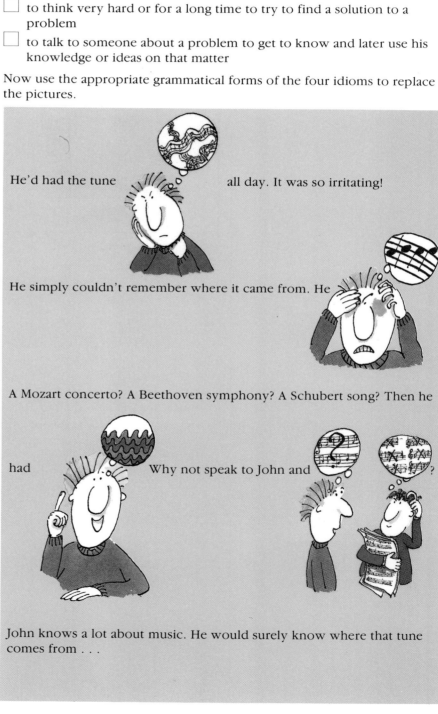

He'd had the tune  all day. It was so irritating!

He simply couldn't remember where it came from. He 

A Mozart concerto? A Beethoven symphony? A Schubert song? Then he had  Why not speak to John and  ?

John knows a lot about music. He would surely know where that tune comes from . . .

Memory

1

What do these expressions mean?

'It's on the tip of my tongue.'

'My head's like a sieve.'

'My mind's gone blank.'

'In one ear and out the other.'

Do you have expressions like these in your language?

2 **Find someone who . . .**

As you do this exercise, walk round the class and talk to as many people as possible. When you *find someone who* . . . write his/her name in the 'names' column below. Find as many *different* names as possible.

	Find someone who can recall . . .	**Names**
1	what they had for dinner last night	....
2	what they were wearing last Tuesday	....
3	the year Christopher Columbus discovered North America	....
4	the year the first man landed on the moon	....
5	the names of all the students in this class	....
6	what they dreamt about last night	....
7	what 'my head's like a sieve' means	....
8	the opening bars of Beethoven's Fifth Symphony	....
9	the smell of onions	....
10	an occasion when they hurt their foot	....
11	which US president preceded Ronald Reagan	....
12	where they were on January 1st	....

3

Discuss *how* you recalled different things in Exercise 2.

4

Read the first four paragraphs of the chapter 'The Psychology of Memory' from *The Brain Book* by Peter Russell. Try to write a definition of 'memory'.

THE PSYCHOLOGY OF MEMORY

Memory is undoubtedly one of the most important human faculties. Without it there would be no learning from experience, no intellectual functioning, no development of language, nor any of the qualities that are generally associated with being human. Yet, with the possible exception of consciousness itself, memory remains the most mysterious of the mind's faculties. Despite the fact that more research has been devoted to the study of memory than to any other mental function, comparatively little is known about how the mind remembers things, and why it also appears to forget.

Memory is often thought of as the ability to recall past events. If someone were asked to remember what he ate for lunch yesterday, he would probably be able to give a brief description, and if we were to check back with what he had actually eaten, it would be possible to see how well he had 'remembered' it.

Memory, however, is more than just the ability to recall. If the same person were asked what he ate for lunch a year ago, he would probably be very unlikely to recall it. Yet if we could remind him of what he actually ate, he might well say, 'Ah yes, now I remember.' He would recognize the items and could still be said to have retained some memory of the event. Thus retention does not necessarily imply recall.

If, after reminding him of an event or situation – in this case a luncheon – he still failed to recognize it, this would not necessarily mean that he had no memory of it. It might well happen that under hypnosis he would be able to recall details of the meal perfectly. There may be many events and experiences that are recorded in memory but that cannot immediately be recalled or recognized. Indeed, there is growing evidence that the brain may record everything that is ever experienced.

5

As you read this section, look back at Exercise 2 *Find someone who . . .*

1 Which types of memory did you use while doing the exercise?
2 Which types of memory described in this section did you *not* use in the exercise?

THE VARIETIES OF MEMORABLE EXPERIENCES

Memory can be divided into several different types:

Episodic Memory. The memory for past episodes and events in one's life, such as tripping over the cat.

Factual Memory. The memory for facts, such as that the Battle of Hastings took place in 1066, or that Einstein formulated the theory of relativity. These are not actual episodes in one's life, though they will have been learned as the result of numerous little episodes at school, in reading, and at other times.

Semantic Memory. The memory for meaning. We remember that a 'butterfly' is an insect with four large brightly colored wings, and that 'smooth' describes a certain tactile sensation, as well as having several other meanings. The average person remembers several hundred thousand words and meanings.

continued

Sensory Memory. Most people have a strong visual memory, being able, whether they believe it or not, to remember several thousand faces, probably seeing most of them clearly 'in the mind's eye'. Many will also be able to remember the sound of favorite pieces of music, or the smell of some tasty dish.

Skills. Skills also involve memory. A person remembers how to get dressed, drive a car, or throw a ball. Even walking and speaking are skills learned early on in life.

Instinctive Memory. The newborn baby 'remembers' to suck at its mother's breast, and the adult brain 'remembers' how to breathe, sleep, digest, etc. The bases of many such memories are inherited and stored in the genes. This genetic memory also specifies many individual characteristics, both physical and mental.

Collective Memory. Psychologists such as Carl Jung have suggested that we may also have access to collective race memories. These appear, mainly in dreams, as archetypal symbols that are very similar for large numbers of people, though outside their normal experience of life.

Past-Life Memory. Some people appear to be able to 'remember' events from before their birth, sometimes from many centuries before. Under hypnosis it is possible to examine this phenomenon more fully, and it is often found that the 'memories' do correlate with actual happenings in the life of an individual in the past – though the subject may have no knowledge of that individual's existence.

There is hardly a moment in our lives when memory is not playing a crucial role, and the more we understand how it functions, the more we can help ourselves at work, at home, in play, and in study, both with others and on our own.

6

Do this experiment as instructed in the text.

AN EXPERIMENT

Before going on to investigate how memory works, it will be useful for you to perform a simple experiment. The results will illustrate several important factors in memory. First, find yourself a pencil or something else to write with. Then read through the following list of words just once. Do not study them, just read each to yourself:

water, life, dog, line, home, mouse,
field, balls, rabbit, apple, sheep, head,
bone, year, goat, Maharishi, hill,
oar, donkey, shape, crop, wind, pig,
tool, cow, door, stone, flower, cat.

On page 39 you will find a blank space. Write there as many of the words as you can remember, in whatever order they come to you. (If you feel bad about writing in books, a sheet of paper will do.)

7 Read the discussion of results in the next section and discuss your own results with the rest of the class.

PRIMACY AND RECENCY

You are unlikely to have recalled the whole of the list (for those who have, we shall be dealing with photographic memory shortly). Among the words that you have written down you will probably find that there are more from the beginning and end of the list. You are more likely to have recalled *water*, *life*, *flower*, and *cat* than *year* and *wind*. The increased probability of recalling the first two or three items is called the *primacy effect*; and that of recalling the last few items is called the *recency effect*. The two effects are shown together in Figure 1, in what is called a serial position curve.

The exact shape of the curve depends on a number of variables, such as the length of the list, the nature of the list – whether it is words, pictures, prose, or the learning of skills – and how much the person organizes the material to be learned and thereby improves memory throughout. In some cases primacy is the strongest effect, in others recency. In any event, the general finding that the beginning and end of a learning session are remembered better occurs again and again in many different learning situations.

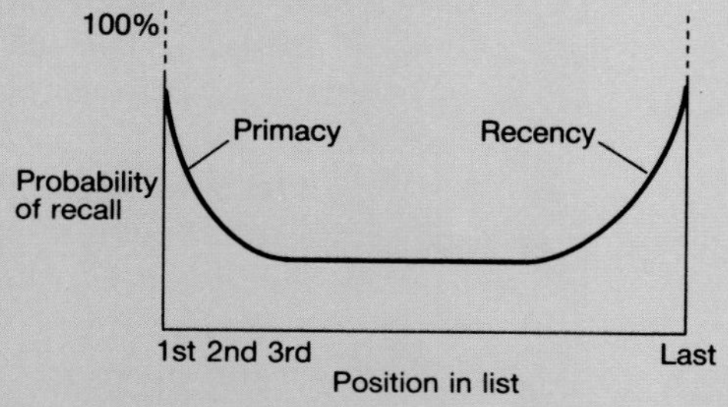

The primacy and recency effects are two factors that enhance the value of taking breaks. A single period of learning benefits from primacy and recency only at the start and finish. If the session is broken into a number of smaller blocks, with short breaks in between, there are more times at which primacy and recency effects can occur.

THE VON RESTORFF EFFECT

In the memory experiment you did earlier most of you will have recalled *Maharishi* – it stood out from the rest of the list. This tendency to remember outstanding elements in a list is called the von Restorff effect.

You may possibly find that you also remembered the words *goat* and *hill* – words positioned on either side of *Maharishi*. The higher arousal created by the outstanding word also effects the retention of those words close to it in the learning sequence. Thus the serial position curve of Figure 2 can be modified to include high retention for outstanding items and their neighbors:

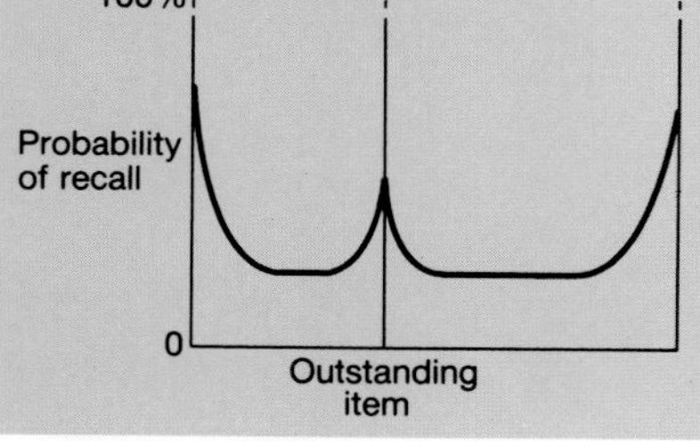

8 Before you read the final section, discuss how you can apply what you have just read about memory to your learning of English.

APPLICATIONS AND ADVICE

Breaks. Any period of study or learning is best broken down into smaller chunks, with short breaks between each session. The actual size of each chunk will depend upon the type of material being studied. In practice, it is found that somewhere between fifteen and forty-five minutes is the best. If the chunk becomes too small, there is not sufficient meaning and internal coherence to gain a proper understanding of the material, and if it is too large, the full benefit of taking breaks is lost.

As to the question of how long the break should be, something of the order of five to ten minutes is best. It has been found that learning improves when the time between blocks is increased from thirty seconds to ten minutes, but no further improvement is gained by increasing the break period further.

During the breaks themselves you should take a complete rest from the type of work under study. If you merely switch to something similar, not only is the mind not given a real break, but numerous interfering associations will be made that will impede later recall. The best thing to do is to relax both mentally and physically and take some fresh air. The rest also helps the mind consolidate and organize the information gained, and it is important to let it get on with this in its own way.

The von Restorff Effect. This can be used to improve memory in a number of ways. Whenever you want to remember something, deliberately make the idea *stand out*.

- Exaggerate it. The more bizarre an idea is, the more arousing it is, and the more clear will be the memory.
- In writing or note taking, use outlining, bold print, colour, and anything else that will make important points stand out.
- When reading, underline important points.
- Everything is unique. Emphasize its uniqueness in your mind, how it is different from everything else.

From *The Brain Book* by Peter Russell (Routledge and Kegan Paul)

9 Exploring 'memory'

Use a monolingual dictionary or a lexicon (e.g. *The Longman Lexicon of Contemporary English* by Tom McArthur) to explore the meanings of the words below. Check:

the pronunciation and stress
the meaning(s) of each word and the overlap of meaning(s) between words
common collocations

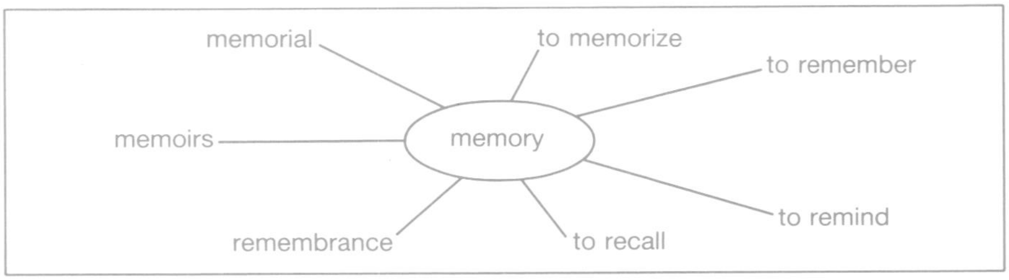

What does the prefix *re* mean (as in *remember*)?

Rewrite the words in your notebook or vocabulary book, using any technique you like that you feel will help you remember the meanings.

10

Complete the table with the correct parts of speech.

Verbs	Nouns	Adjectives
to retain		
to recognize		
to impede		——
——	episode	
	sensation	
to taste		
——	fact	
to digest		
to stand out	——	
——		genetic
		visual
	emphasis	

11

Practise using the words in the table above and any other words that you wish to review from the text by playing the 'coffee-pot' game.

1 Think of a sentence that illustrates the meaning of the word you want to review.
2 Say the sentence to the rest of the class, using *coffee-pot* instead of the word you are reviewing.
3 The other students must guess what the word is, e.g.
Student A: I have a very good coffee-pot memory. I always remember faces.
Student B: Visual.

How Creative are You?

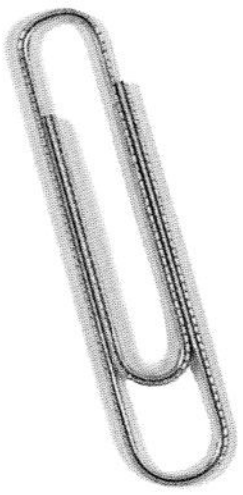

1 Here is a standard *creativity test* that is used in schools, colleges and large business organizations.

Give yourself *exactly two minutes* to write down, as fast as you can, all the different uses you can think of for an ordinary paperclip.

Score yourself:
Add up the total number of uses you thought of. Divide this number by two. This will give you an average number of uses thought of per minute.

What do you think of this test? (The average score ranges between 2 and 8.) Does it measure some aspect(s) of your creativity?

2 The author of the text below does not think that the test you have just done is a valid one. He thinks the test has two main faults. What are these?

Creativity

Creativity, of all the mental areas, is that one in which most people rank themselves especially low. This is not surprising, because the 'creative brain', for want of a better expression, is generally left out of education. Any activity which involves imagination, colour, rhythm, or form has been traditionally frowned upon as 'less intelligent'. Fortunately we now have more information to work with, and creativity can be seen as a necessary part of a well-balanced education and personality.

The test which you have just done is one of the traditional tests given to measure this aspect of our intellect. The faults of this test were of two main kinds. First, it assumed creative ability to be simply quantitative – i.e. dependent on the *number* of uses a person could think of; and secondly, even in the quantitative area it was weak. It did not actually measure the 'basic' or 'innate' capacities that it purported to measure – that is, creativity. Instead it measured how inadequately the brain had been taught to combine language and imagination.

All that the test measures is the rigidity with which the person being tested has been taught to use language, especially words like 'uses'. The more rigidly taught mind will assume that 'uses' refers to ordinary sensible applications of a paperclip. The less rigidly taught mind, and the one which consequently will be regarded as more creative, will find more expansive interpretations of the word 'uses', and consequently will come up with many more applications for the paperclip. The creative genius will break all the ordinary boundaries, and will include in his list many 'far out' applications such as melting a few million of them down to form the shell of a space-ship.

The creative mind is expanding his connections for the word 'uses' to include the phrase 'connections with'.

Realizing that this is the proper method of performing in a creativity test, and remembering that the mind can make a virtually limitless series of connections, linking any one thing to anything else, we realize that our score can immediately go off the top of the chart.

From *Make the Most of Your Mind* by Tony Buzan (Pan Books)

3 Look at the list of 40 items below. In pairs or small groups, give yourselves *five minutes* to see how many associations you can make between the items and the idea of a paperclip.

'For some of these you will be able to find connections immediately, others may at first seem obscure and impossible. In the end you will find they can all be connected to "paperclip" in some way, as did the person who connected them all except "pigeon". This he was convinced had no connection, until a friend suggested using a paperclip to fix an important message on to the pigeon's leg.' (Buzan, *ibid.*)

orange	lightbulb	pigeon	cloud
wood	tea	pub	watch
handbag	kitchen	pepper	rain
tree	banana	window	pen
bottle	glass	water	house
mirror	leaf	tyre	shoe
chair	holiday	wine	table
ear	book	garden	dinner
maid	radio	potato	cup
Germany	garage	newspaper	

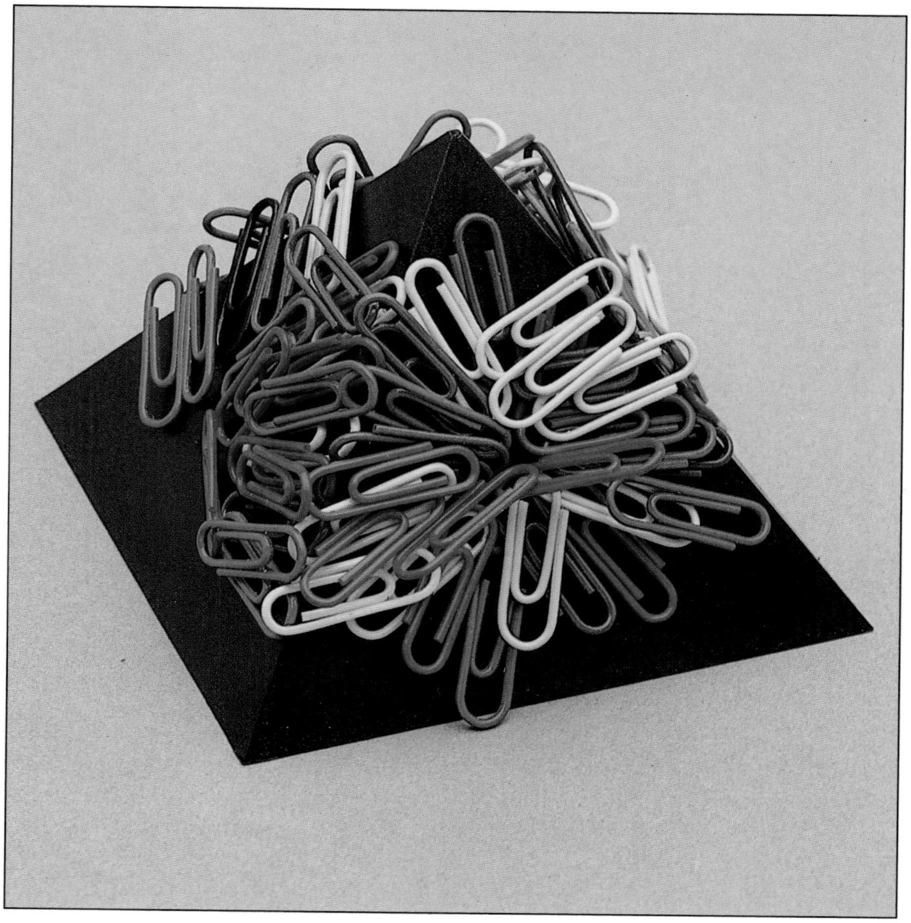

5 Work

Work Proverbs

All work and no play makes Jack a dull boy.

Describe someone to whom you feel you could apply this proverb.

Many hands make light work.

Is this always true? Give some examples of when it is/when it isn't true.

A bad workman always blames his tools.

Have you ever been guilty of 'blaming your tools'?

Career Counselling

Many people are happy with the career they have chosen. But there are others who feel they are following a career that does not altogether suit them. How well a particular career suits you depends partly on how well it matches your interests and the values you hold.

1

Here is a list of occupational interests that has been drawn up by a psychologist.

1 Match each interest with an appropriate definition. The first one has been done for you.
2 Choose two interests that are important to you. Are they reflected in the career you have chosen? Explain your choice to a partner.

Occupational interests

1 scientific	☐	working with tools and materials
2 computational	1	investigating physical and biological phenomena to understand why and how things happen
3 artistic	☐	concerning yourself with helping others
4 persuasive	☐	dealing with figures
5 practical	☐	expressing ideas and feelings through words
6 literary	☐	influencing others to accept your goods, ideas and services
7 welfare	☐	creating and appreciating things of beauty

2

Here is a list of values and attitudes. Again, it has been drawn up by a psychologist.

1 Match each value or attitude with an appropriate definition.
2 Choose two values that are particularly important to you. Are they reflected in the career you have chosen? Explain your choice to a partner.

Values and attitudes

1 intellectual	☐	seeking beauty and harmony in all forms and media
2 aesthetic	☐	seeking practical means to achieve economic progress
3 power	☐	searching for the truth through academic investigations
4 religious	☐	seeking ways of helping other people for their own sake
5 material	☐	seeking and competing for positions of power and authority
6 altruistic	☐	seeking spiritual rather than material satisfaction

3 Jonathan Elford is a university lecturer in his mid-thirties. He is not altogether happy with his present job but cannot decide what alternative career he might pursue. Recently he decided to ask a career-counselling service for advice.

What do you think the career-counselling service did to find out more about Jonathan and to help him?

On the cassette you can hear an interview with Jonathan. As you listen make notes in answer to these questions.

1 Make a list of the things the career-counselling service did. Beside each activity, note down its purpose.

Activity	Purpose
1	
2	
3	
4	

2 What were some of the questions that Jonathan was asked?
3 Did Jonathan find the career counselling helpful? Why?/Why not?

4 What kind of help were *you* given in choosing a career?

Job Satisfaction

1 Read this list of factors that can contribute to job satisfaction:

a high salary
lots of perks, e.g. a company car, travel expenses
good promotion prospects
an opportunity, through your job, to serve others in the community/in society
a pleasant, friendly working atmosphere
short working hours – not more than 35 hours a week
long holidays

2 Add any other factors that you think should be included in the list.

3 How important is each factor for you? Number them in order of importance, starting with 1 = the most important.

4 In pairs compare your numbering. Try to discuss each factor, giving reasons why you have given it that number.

5 These phrases are often used in the context of jobs:

to climb the ladder
to move to the next rung

What do you think they mean?

Life at the Bottom

1 Look at the photograph and the title of the article. Try to predict what the article is about.

2 Skim-read the article. Is your prediction correct?

3 Read the article quickly. Do not worry about understanding every word at this stage. As you read, complete the table below.

Marian Thiel	1976	2 years ago	now
Job			
Salary			
Town			

Sunday Times

Life at the bottom:

Hard-up, tired but content

To most people, changing jobs means stepping up the ladder: more money, a higher position, travel perhaps, more perks, the next rung on the way to a so-called better life. So why change?

Marian Thiel has been changing jobs ever since she first started working at the age of 18 when she was a sales assistant in a fashion store in Bristol. She had left school with three O-levels – Art, English, Needlework. By 1976, at the age of 31, she was senior executive in charge of public relations at Chester Barrie, a fashion menswear house based in Crewe. She was on a salary of £4,500 – plus perks. She had a secretary, a company car and first-class travel expenses. She went to the hairdresser once a week (paid for, of course) and on the strength of her job and prospects had got herself a three-bedroomed semi on the river at Congleton.

"I used to have my nails painted just to look better," she says now, almost in disbelief, "and I used to take taxis everywhere so my hair didn't get wet or blown about. I was out every day for lunch or dinner with customers. I was out of the office on business four days out of five, very often in London, France or Germany. If I went to Scotland, I flew – and there was always a chauffeur and car to meet me."

About two years ago she gave it all up to become a nurse. Her pay during her first year as a student State Registered Nurse at St. Stephen's Hospital, London, was £90 a month: £74 of that went back to Cheshire to pay for her mortgage. Suddenly she was living off £16 a month – and *no* expenses. "I used to walk along the streets of Westminster crying," she says. "Of course it was *my* decision not to let the house go – just because you make a break you don't have to give up everything."

She has now moved back to her house in Congleton in Cheshire, having transferred to a local hospital for the last year of her training. The pay is a bit better now – £140 a month with overtime – but the hours are long and she finds the work physically exhausting. There are certainly no trips to the hairdresser, no spending sprees.

So why did she do it? What happened to the normal job pattern? She is patently not someone who has just opted out of the rat-race. She admits she loves the good life, and offered the chance of a job at £10,000 tomorrow, she would jump at it. "I could pick up and live again as though I had never been poor," she says. But, she goes on, she feels we all have a debt to society. "It's rather like the land," she says. "The times we are living in now are very materialistic, everyone's on the make, everything's got to be brighter and newer. We're all taking things out and never putting back. And what happens if you do that to the land? You get barren soil. I certainly never wanted to be a nurse, but I realized that I had to give instead of just take." *Victoria Hainworth*

4 Read the article more carefully. As you read, mark the statements below T (True), F (False) or NS (Not sure).

1 Marian Thiel felt appearance was important in her job as senior executive.
2 It was not easy for her to make the change from senior executive to student nurse.
3 She can now easily afford her house in Congleton.
4 She finds nursing extremely rewarding.
5 In the exercise on Job Satisfaction above, she would probably list as most important 'an opportunity, through your job, to serve others in the community/in society'.

5 In pairs, compare your answers to Exercise 4 and discuss any differences.

6 Here are some possible titles for the article, and the original title. Which one do you think is best? Why? (Your reasons may be related to length; style; how well it summarizes the article, etc.)

FROM TOP TO BOTTOM: GIVING INSTEAD OF TAKING

Down the Ladder – From Senior Executive to Student Nurse

Money isn't everything

MARIAN THIEL'S DEBT TO SOCIETY

Life at the bottom: Hard-up, tired but content

7 Do you think you could ever be like Marian Thiel – willingly choose to step down the ladder instead of up?

8 As you learned in Unit 4, the more we can use *both* sides of the brain, the more efficient our learning will be. This applies to the learning of new vocabulary: if you try to *visualize* a new word, you will probably remember it better.

1 Without looking back, can you 'see' in your mind's eye the picture of the ladder at the beginning of the section on Job Satisfaction? What vocabulary does it illustrate?

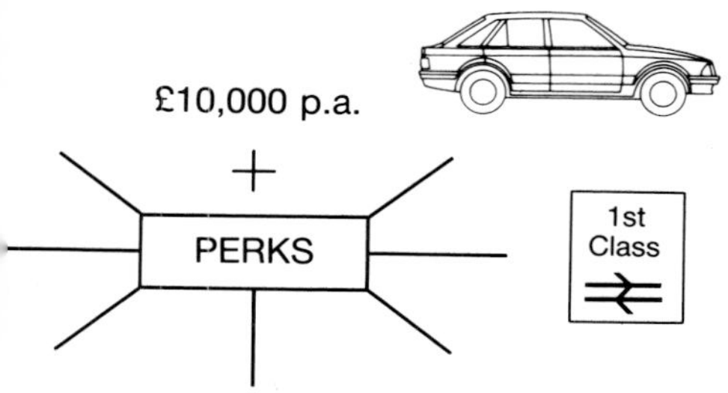

2 *perks*, which was in the reading text, may have been a new word for you. On the left is one attempt to visualize it. Add other pictures to illustrate other perks, e.g. a free telephone, hairdressing, luncheon vouchers. Share and explain your drawings to your neighbours.

3 Make drawings to help you visualize these words and phrases:

hard up
spending spree
a three-bedroomed semi
to promote (promotion)

Walk around the class and look at other students' drawings. Explain your drawings to each other.

9

The reading text used the noun *a perk*. *perk* can also be used as a verb *to perk up* and an adjective *perky*, as in these sentences:

He *perked up* when he heard the good news.
She's a *perky* little thing.

Use a monolingual dictionary to find out the meaning of *to perk up* and *perky*.

10

Use a monolingual dictionary to explore the meanings of *break* and *bottom*, as used in these phrases and sentences.

break **to make a break**
to give someone a break
a lucky break

bottom **from the bottom of my heart**
to knock the bottom out of an argument
He's a good fellow at bottom.
The bottom has fallen out of the market.

Illustrate some of these meanings with quick drawings. Share your drawings with your neighbours.

What's My Line?

This game can be played in pairs, or in small groups. The aim of the game is to find out by asking questions what your opponent's occupation is.

1 Student A invents an occupation for himself/herself, e.g. plumber, travel agent.
2 The other student(s) must find out what A's occupation is by asking questions. Student A will answer either YES or NO, so the questions must be formulated carefully. Keep a record of how many questions are used to discover A's occupation.
3 Take it in turns to be A.
If you are playing in pairs, the player using the fewest questions is the winner. If you are playing in small groups, the player who causes the other players to use most questions is the winner.

The Selection Board

Role-play

Work in small groups. The group is the selection board of St Peter's Hospital, Crewe.

Recently you put this advertisement in *Nursing News*:

STAFF NURSE

A dedicated, committed staff nurse is required to work as part of a small team of doctors, psychologists and nurses in a newly established women's geriatric unit at St. Peter's Hospital, Crewe. Experience in this kind of work is less important than an imaginative approach, the ability to learn quickly, a commitment to hard work, the ability to work as part of a team and great patience.

Salary: £7,500 – £8,350 p.a.

Apply to: Personnel, St. Peter's Hospital, Crewe

There are four applicants for the post: Marian Thiel and three others.

1 Read the information about the applicants and look back at the article about Marian Thiel to refresh your memory.
2 Decide which of the four applicants should get the job.
3 Report your choice and the reasons for it to the rest of the class.

PETER SYMONDS

Peter, 23, appears to be very bright and critical. He went to York University at the age of 18 to study Chemistry, but he dropped out after a year and spent 18 months working in a small children's home, where he was given quite a lot of responsibility. Peter then did his nursing training in London, finishing last year, since when he has been working in a children's ward.

He recently got married, and his wife is now pregnant. He's looking for a bigger flat.

JOANNE BLAKE

Joanne, 22, was a very bright student at school, finishing with A-level passes in Geography, English and Biology. She went straight to Nursing School and has just finished her course.

She's interested in this job although she would prefer, in the long term, to work with children.

While on the nursing course she met a young doctor. They are now engaged.

BRIGIT GRIFFITHS

Brigit, 27, has been a nurse for the last eight years; it has been her only job. She has had some experience with geriatric medicine. She is Canadian. She has been living in England for just over a year. In Canada she completed her secondary school education as an average student.

She seems very strong-willed and possibly quick-tempered.

6 School

Attitudes to Education

In 1984 the *Observer Sunday Magazine* conducted a survey of attitudes of British people to children's education.

1 Read the survey questions below and answer them. Then, in pairs, compare and discuss your answers.

Attitudes to Education

For each of the questions 1–4, put a tick (✓) in the box that indicates your answer.

1 Which one of the following groups do you think should have the greatest influence in deciding what is taught in each school?

- The Government ☐
- Local authorities ☐
- Parent groups ☐
- Teachers ☐
- Don't know ☐

2 Do you think girls are better off going to single-sex or mixed schools?

- Single-sex schools ☐
- Mixed schools ☐
- Don't know ☐

3 Do you think boys are better off going to single-sex or mixed schools?

- Single-sex schools ☐
- Mixed schools ☐
- Don't know ☐

4 How strongly do you agree or disagree that 'It is not as important for girls to go to college or university as for boys'?

- Strongly agree ☐
- Agree fairly strongly ☐
- Disagree fairly strongly ☐
- Disagree very strongly ☐
- Don't know ☐

5 **(a)** Which three of these subjects are the most important at school nowadays?
(b) Which three of these subjects are the least important?

Put ticks in the appropriate columns to indicate your choices.

Most Important		Least Important
	social studies	
	history	
	computer studies	
	sex education	
	peace studies	
	business studies	
	science	
	foreign languages	
	religious education	
	geography	
	art	
	technical subjects	
	home economics	
	mathematics	
	economics	
	woodwork/metalwork	
	mother tongue	
	physical education	

2 Find out how each question has been answered by all the students in the class.

For questions 1–4, count how many students used each possible answer.

For question 5, for each subject count how many students marked it as (a) the most important, and (b) the least important.

3 On page 103 you will find the results of the British survey. Compare them with the results of your class survey.

The Ideal Teacher

1 Look at the list of possible attributes of an ideal teacher.

1 Add any other attributes you think are important.
2 Number from 1 to 5 the five attributes that you think are most important.
3 In pairs, compare your choices and discuss them.

The ideal teacher . . .
is strict
dresses well
is good-looking
doesn't have pets
has a sense of humour
knows how to maintain discipline in the class
is young
respects pupils
is a good listener
is fair and just to all pupils
is kind
. . . . .
. . . . .
. . . . .
. . . . .
. . . . .
. . . . .
. . . . .
. . . . .

2 On the cassette you will hear four teenagers giving their ideas about the ideal teacher. You will first hear Laura, Nicola and Tracey, who live and go to school in Reading, forty miles west of London. You will also hear Jillian, who is Tracey's elder sister. She has just left school and goes to Reading Technical College.

1 As you listen, take notes about the attributes that the teenagers think are important. Listen once without stopping. Then listen again, stopping and starting as necessary for more detailed understanding.
2 Do you agree with the teenagers' opinions?

3 If you were a teacher, which age group would you choose to teach? Why? Which subjects would you choose? Why?

The School that I'd Like

1 In December 1967 *The Observer* newspaper invited secondary school children to enter for a competition. They were to describe 'The School that I'd Like'. Here is one of the competition entries, written by William, aged 15. He describes two contrasting history lessons.

1 Which lesson is most similar to history lessons you have had at school?
2 In the school that he'd like, what is William's attitude to . . .
discipline?
teaching methods?
teacher – pupil relationships?

Johnny crashed through the garden gate and stormed down the path, demolishing some of his father's prize blooms with his trailing satchel. Finding his way blocked by the front door, he sank on to a paving stone and announced to the whole neighbourhood, 'I 'ATE SCOOW!'

Johnny is by no means unique. Thousands of boys and girls throughout this country feel the same way towards this compulsory purgatory.

If Britain is to hold its own in the technological and artistic world of tomorrow, she must educate her children thoroughly and, above all, in an interesting way.

A history lesson in Johnny's school would probably go something as follows:

Lookout at the door of the classroom sees teacher approach, and tells the class to 'Belt up, it's coming!' *Sudden quiet. The teacher enters. Class rises.*

Teacher	Good morning, children.
Class	Good morning, sir.
Teacher	Sit down and get your exercise books out. Today I'll dictate.
Class	Oh, not again!
Teacher	Be quiet, or you'll have to stay behind tonight. Now, get your pens ready. What is it, Smith?
Johnny	Please, sir, my pen has no ink.
Teacher	Well, fill it. Had only been on the throne for a few –
Johnny	Please, sir, I didn't catch that last piece,
Teacher	Leave a space and copy it later. A few months. William, Duke of Normandy –
Johnny	Please sir, my nib's broken.
Teacher	Stop interrupting my lesson, Smith, and stand outside the room for the rest of the period!

continued

At the end of that lesson, Johnny would know next to nothing of the events of 1066, and after a few more lessons like that, he would lose interest in the subject, and his mind would slowly dull.

Ideally, the schools of tomorrow should keep the minds of their pupils active. The best way to accomplish this is to allow the children to take more part in the lessons. They should discuss the subject they are learning with the teacher, airing their own views and listening to other pupils'.

The atmosphere should be less formal, the teachers calling both boys and girls by their Christian names, the classes being smaller, and the lessons becoming less and less like lessons, and more like debates.

A history lesson in these circumstances would go this way:

The teacher enters and the class rises.

Teacher Good morning.
Class Good morning, sir.
Teacher Now, today I thought we should leave the actual course of the Napoleonic Wars, and concentrate on Napoleon as a man. Has anyone any views on the subject?
Johnny In the last lesson you said that Napoleon was a megalomaniac. I don't think he was.
Teacher Can you back that up, John?
Johnny In the first place, he didn't really want to . . . and so I don't think he was exalting himself.
Teacher That was very interesting, John. I know there are only eleven of us here, but surely someone disagrees with what John said. What's your view, Elizabeth?
Elizabeth Well, I think that . . .

I should think that a vast majority of today's school children would prefer to be taught in a school using the second method, but will probably not get the chance.

William, 15

From *The School that I'd Like*, edited by Edward Blishen (Penguin)

2 Discuss the school that you'd like (or would have liked).

If you are still at school:
1 What do you like about school? Why?
2 What do you not like about school? Why?
3 What do you think the aims of secondary education should be?
4 What changes would you like to make in your school?
5 Describe the school that you'd like to have and make a list of the kind of changes that you'd like.

If you are no longer at school:
1 What did you like about school? Why?
2 What did you not like about school? Why?
3 What do you think the aims of secondary education should be?
4 What changes would you like to have made in your school?
5 Describe the school that you'd have liked to have had and make a list of the kind of changes that you'd have liked.

3 Here is another competition entry, written in the form of a poem by Melanie, a 14-year-old girl. Read it and make a list of the changes that Melanie would like to make to school. Compare this list with the list you made in Exercise 2.

Step with me into a future school.
I'll show you around.
Even at a glance you've found
Things very different and strange.
– Where are the clouds of white dust
From the scraping chalk?
Nobody sits on wooden chairs, at wooden desks,
Listening to teachers talk.
The framed blackboard is nowhere to be seen.
Everything is clean.
The rooms are bright,
And large, and wide, and very light.

No one minds what we wear.
Clothes aren't considered important,
So usually our feet are bare.
No one minds about anything much, really.
There is no whisper
Of engraved desks, arranged in ranks.
Or uniforms.
How could you bear
The drabness? Didn't you care
That each child was an echo
Of his neighbour?

We study at school for three days each week.
For the last hour of the third day
We hold discussions, in groups.
We talk on many things,
From religion to politics,
To our own personal problems.
We discuss human relationships,
And we look back, and see
What happened when knowledge gave man power.
Then we realize the importance
Of wisdom, as well.
– These discussions are led
By a student who is studying
For A.O.Es.
(Those are the Advanced Oral Exams.
When a pupil has taken one,
He writes a thesis on their improvement.
Not many people are bright enough
To take them all. I won't be.
You have to be really clever, you see.)

It is a good school.
Hard work, sometimes,
But people always lend
A hand.
I can depend on someone
To help me understand.
There is so much to learn
That I will only touch the edge of it –
And simply sift the sand.
– If I had a good brain
I would dig really deep, and learn.

continued

But I am not shaped for that.
I have as much to give
As the bright ones.
I know how to live
Even if I never reach second in command.
I have my purpose, too.
If we were all brilliant,
Who would be the crew?

There is a lot for me to do
To prepare me for whatever is in store.
But although I am a student and I learn,
I am not preparing for life.
I am alive now.
Learning is the start of something stretching before me,
And my heart
Says it will be great.
But I can wait.
This present learning tense suits me all right,
Although I'm not too bright.

Melanie, 14

From *The School that I'd Like*, edited by Edward Blishen (Penguin)

Ask the Right Question

The aim of this game is to review vocabulary by asking questions that will elicit the vocabulary under review.

1 Work in small groups of three or four.
2 Your teacher will give each group a pile of small cards. Each card has a word or phrase that the teacher would like you to review. Place the pile of cards FACE DOWN in the middle of the group.
3 Student A picks up the top card and shows it to everyone in the group *except the person on his/her left (Student B).* Anyone in the group now asks Student B a question aimed at getting him/her to say the word on the card. If the first question does not get the word on the card, the group continues asking more questions until Student B says the word.
4 Continue playing the game in the same way, taking it in turns to be Students A and B.

Rural Schools

1 Dotted around the British Isles are several tiny rural primary schools with only one teacher and a few pupils. Below is a list of characteristics of small rural schools. Discuss each characteristic and decide whether it constitutes an advantage or a drawback. Add any others to the list that you can think of.

Characteristics of small rural schools

The children:
- have a flexible timetable
- get individual attention
- enjoy few facilities, e.g. for sport, science etc.
- live near the school
- have few playmates of the same age and sex
- have the world of nature on their school doorstep

From *The Observer*

2

Now read the article 'Small-Scale Schools'. As you read it:

1 label each school on the map of the British Isles below.
2 for each school, name the single most important advantage the pupils appear to have.

Small-Scale Schools

Imagine being in a school with only two or three pupils. HELEN PICKLES reports

Mousonmere Beach, Herm.

Rhum

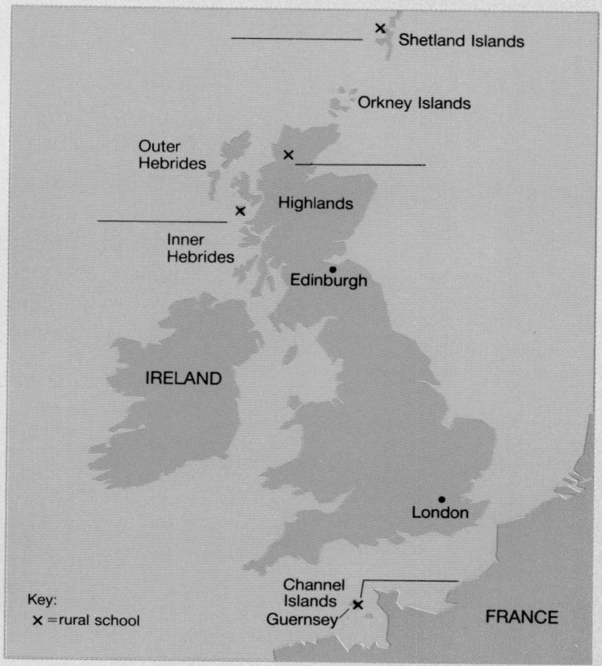

HERM

'In cities it takes a long time to walk to school, but it only takes me 30 seconds,' claimed Sarah Osborne, 7. Her schoolteacher has the longest journey – a 12-minute hike up the hill. And that's a long walk on an island only 1½ miles long by ½ mile wide. Herm Island (pop. 40), is one of the smallest Channel Islands: 'There aren't any roads to cross because there aren't any cars.' Pupils on small islands have definite advantages, said Ann Scholl, 5: 'At a big school they have a hall where they do games but here we go down to the beach.'

'We can easily go and see all the wild life,' agreed Gareth Murray, 10. 'Curlews, puffins and oystercatchers, for example, then we come back to school and write about them.'

Once a week, the six pupils go to a school on Guernsey and join a class of their own age group, but the best part is the boat journey there and back. Said 7-year-old Russell Swann: 'I like it when we come back and it's rough, but my teacher hates it.'

SUTHERLAND

If Mary Ann, 6, turns up at school just 5 seconds late, it's immediately noticed. When teacher Mrs Jolly asks the class a question she always looks at Mary Ann. When you're the only pupil in the school there's not a great deal you can do.

Mary Ann Grant's father is a keeper on a remote Highland estate in Sutherland. There isn't a school nearby so the education authority decided to give her her own teacher and schoolroom. 'I thought it would be the easiest job I had ever done,' said Mrs Jolly, 'but that soon changed. I have to take the part of another pupil, really, and it can be very exhausting. We don't have a timetable, as such. We might be doing arithmetic and suddenly a bird appears at the window, so we start a discussion about that.' Mrs Jolly is also learning things from Mary Ann: 'She teaches me about the stags and also tells me some of the Highland folklore.'

RHUM

'There's only one classroom in our school because the room next door is used as the church.' Sandra Mackay, 10, has just five classmates at her school on the Hebridean island of Rhum. This whole island is a nature reserve so red deer, feral goats and grey seals are a common sight. The pupils know they're lucky but small schools have their drawbacks.

'I like this school, but I do miss other boys to play with,' said Peter Mackay, the only boy in the school. Sports are also a problem. 'We have to improvise a lot,' said teacher Miss McMullen. 'We play badminton in the community hall, but the ceiling's a bit low.'

'Sometimes we go out in Land-Rovers,' said Beth Johnson. 'There are no cars here, the roads are too stony. Recently we went to look at a "shieling" where the crofting women lived in the summer to look after the sheep.'

PAPA STOUR

On Papa Stour – just off Shetland – the days are much shorter in winter so, when it gets dark, the school lessons finish for the day. The timetable has to alter with the seasons because the island is so far north. The six pupils, aged 4 to 8, are each given separate work to do for most subjects. 'But the timetable is very flexible and tends to fit around TV and radio programmes,' said teacher Mrs Buggy. Her husband helps out by teaching art, and he is also the school cook specialising in pizzas.

What do the pupils miss most on the island? 'Ice-cream!' they all cried. 'It has to come from the mainland and by the time it gets here it's melted.'

3 Would you like to have been a pupil in a small rural school? Why/Why not?

4 Would you like to be a teacher in one of the schools described in the article? Why/Why not?

School Closure

Role-play

The Situation

Because of recent government cuts in the education budget, the Channel Islands Council wishes to close the Primary School on Herm Island. Most of the islanders are against the proposal. The Channel Islands Education Department has called a meeting with island representatives and the head teacher of a primary school on Guernsey to discuss the problem and to decide what should be done.

The Meeting will be chaired by the Chief Education Officer from the Channel Islands Education Department. He has prepared an agenda for the meeting:

AGENDA

1 Welcome from the Chairman

2 Introductions

3 Chairman's statement on proposed closure of Herm Primary School

4 Statements of island representatives

5 Statement of Guernsey Primary School representative

6 Questions and open discussion

7 Any other business

Roles

Tom Jarrett:	Chief Education Officer
Elizabeth Davies:	principal of a primary school on Guernsey
Janet Hill:	teacher at Herm Primary School
Rosemary Osborne:	mother of a pupil at Herm Primary School
Martin Murray:	father of a pupil at Herm Primary School
Andrew Curtis:	a Herm resident

1 Choose one of the roles and read your role card.
2 Take part in the meeting.
3 Report your group's decision to the rest of the class.

Tom Jarrett

You want to close the school . . .

1 because, although from an educational point of view the children at the school are better off there than at a school on Guernsey, it does not make economic sense to keep the school running
2 because the Council knows that it could sell the land to a travel firm who would build a small hotel on the site.

Elizabeth Davies

You want to close the school . . .

1 because your school will get more pupils, and you will get a little more money for your school – which is already suffering from financial cuts.
2 You would be happy to offer Janet Hill, the teacher, a job.

Janet Hill

You want to keep the school . . .

1 because you would lose your job
2 because you have worked here for 15 years
3 because the children's work would be disrupted
4 because the children cannot make the boat trip every day to Guernsey.

Rosemary Osborne

You want to keep the school . . .

1 because your daughter Sara is happy there
2 because she gets easily seasick on the crossing to Guernsey
3 because she is too young to be a boarder on Guernsey during the week
4 because you went to the school when you were a child.

Martin Murray

You haven't made up your mind yet.

1 Your son Gareth is happy at the school, *but* he is 10 years old and will be going to secondary school on Guernsey next year.
2 Your daughter Sally, aged 8, is a very shy child and you think she might benefit from being with a larger class in a school on Guernsey.
3 You think Janet Hill, the teacher, is very good at her job and you would be sorry for her if she lost it.
4 With no school on Herm, families with young children will not want to stay on the island.

Andrew Curtis

You haven't made up your mind yet.

1 You were at the school when you were a child and were happy there.
2 You admit it is not economic to have a school for so few children, *but* if the school is closed, families with young children will not want to stay on Herm, and there will be no newcomers to the island. You do not want it to become an island of old people.
3 You are 65 years old and your children are all grown up.

Adapted from *Take Five*, by Michael Carrier (Harrap)

7 Business and industry

Difficult Tasks for Managers

1 Read the first three paragraphs of 'Difficult Tasks for Managers', an article from *International Management*. What particular aspect of a manager's role do you think the article is about?

The days when a manager could expect subordinates to jump up from their desks with a courteous 'Good morning, sir!' as he arrived at his office are long past. In the modern world, a manager has to expect subordinates to show less deference.

But the line between the familiarity that comes from more social equality and ill-manners or rudeness is a fine one. And employees who persistently trespass over that line can disrupt an entire department.

How to deal with this type of employee is a delicate problem. The insubordination can be expressed in a variety of subtle ways, most of which are not easy to define in resorting to disciplinary measures.

2 What kinds of behaviour would you consider to be insubordination towards a boss?

3

In the next part of the article, you will read about four problem employees:

Sullen Sally

Tactless Ted

Cartoon Ken

Familiar Fergus

As you read, fill in the blanks with the appropriate names.

Sometimes, people simply do not realize they are being ill-mannered. Take . . . . . , for example. He prides himself on speaking his mind, and has something to say on everything. But his frankness is often acutely embarrassing.

He is incapable of saying, 'I thought that last advertising campaign had a lot of good ideas in it, but perhaps next time we could give the copy more vitality.' Instead, he is apt to blurt out bluntly, 'That campaign was a disaster. A child of three could have done better!'

The fact that he is often right does not help. Other employees resent his manner even more, and he is too insensitive to notice. . . . . .'s bluntness may not be aimed directly at his manager. He is not insensitive enough to call his boss a fool to his face. But the inference is always there that the manager must have had a mental aberration to allow someone to produce such a shoddy piece of work.

Another character among the cast of ill-mannered employees is . . . . . , who seems to regard just being at work as a severe penance. Everything is done begrudgingly. Asking her to do a task beyond her basic job description is often not worth the trouble. It will be done, but only half-heartedly, and her manager will feel the smouldering heat of her resentment on his back a long way down the corridor. If she is asked to make a cup of coffee, she will be certain to slop it in the cup as she deposits it heavily on his desk.

. . . . . is just the opposite. Instead of resentment or aloofness to his boss, he shows a gushing over-familiarity. When an important visitor is shown into the manager's office, ... cannot take the hint and leave. Instead, he will attempt to take part in the conversation, declaring, 'You can talk in front of me. Henry and I don't have many secrets, do we?'

Over the years . . . . . has fallen behind his former equal. But he seeks to maintain the same close relationship that he imagines existed in their younger days.

. . . . . also takes liberties. If the chief executive makes a *faux pas* at an embassy reception, ... will be passing around a limerick on the subject the next morning. If the sales manager breaks his leg skiing, ... will circulate a suitable cartoon of the incident before the plaster sets. He loses no opportunity to poke fun at his superiors, or anyone else for that matter.

4 In small groups discuss how a manager should deal with each of the four problem employees. Draw a table like the one below on a piece of paper and make notes in the left-hand column.

How to deal with difficult employees

	Your suggestions	The author's suggestions
Sullen Sally		
Tactless Ted		
Cartoon Ken		
Familiar Fergus		

5 Read the last part of the article. Fill in the blanks with the appropriate names: Sullen Sally, Tactless Ted, Cartoon Ken, Familiar Fergus.

In the table above make notes in the right-hand column about the author's suggestions for dealing with the four problem employees. Do you agree with the author's suggestions?

It is difficult for most people to be as blunt to . . . . . as he is to others. But no other approach is likely to break through his insensitivity.

Tackling such unpalatable problems is part of a manager's job. . . . . . 's boss needs to steel himself for a heart-to-heart talk in which he explains the demotivating effect that insensitive, tactless comments can have upon other people. Openly recording a staff meeting on tape may provide a manager with the evidence he needs to convince . . . . . of just how rude he is. Then, if a suitable course in human relations is available, he should insist that . . . . enrol, giving him time off to attend.

The truth is that business and friendship often do not mix. Even in highly participative organizations, managers need to maintain a certain distance from their subordinates in order to preserve their authority. A manager must quickly establish that special relationships cannot be tolerated if they upset the smooth running of an office. If that does not work, then ultimately . . . . .'s manager must choose between his career and his friendship.

As long as . . . . . 's activities are harmless and are not upsetting other people, they should be ignored. There is no reason for the executive either openly to condone or curtail these scribblings. But the fact that . . . . . feels inspired to direct creativity into such trivial matters is a sign that it is not being used fully elsewhere. Creative minds are in short supply. . . . . . .'s manager should look for opportunities to divert his energies into more useful areas.

. . . . . is suffering from lack of motivation. Whether her manager can change her attitude depends to a great extent on his abilities in human relations. He can at least try to determine what kind of work . . . . . would like to do and attempt to adapt her job or seek suitable training for her. Praise when she does things well may also help her to get to like her work, as may the simple fact that the manager displays an interest in her job satisfaction and career. Should these measures have no effect, the choice is to suffer her behaviour or to arrange for her departure.

From *International Management*

6

What does *to speak one's mind* mean? (line 12)

Use a monolingual dictionary to find other expressions that use *mind*. Make sentences using the expressions.

What do these expressions mean?

to call someone a fool to his face (line 22)
half-heartedly (line 29)
a heart-to-heart talk (line 51)

7

Here are some other expressions using parts of the body. Use a dictionary to find out what they mean.

to pull someone's leg
to have a finger in every pie
to talk behind someone's back
to keep an eye on something
to not turn a hair
to be a pain in the neck
to keep one's hand in
to make a clean breast of something
to fall on one's feet

Complete these sentences using an appropriate expression from the list above.

1 Would you believe it! The day after he was made redundant he got an offer of a job at twice his old salary. He always seems to . . . .
2 Rather than let his wife find out for herself what he had been up to, he decided it was best to . . . .
3 I really admire him. There he was, guns firing all around him, and he didn't . . . .
4 I can't stand him. He's boring, he interferes all the time – in short, he's . . . .
5 I used to play a lot of bridge. Now I play only occasionally – just to . . . .

8

Now write sentences of your own that illustrate some of the expressions in Exercise 7. Leave a blank where the expression should be. Ask other students to complete your sentences.

Brain teasers

Work in pairs or groups of three and try to solve these brain teasers. Compare your solutions with another group. You can also find the solution on page 104.

1 Mr Smith went to a bank and said, 'If you lend me as much money as I have with me now, I'll deposit £100 with you.' The bank manager agreed and Mr Smith deposited the money.

He then went to a second bank and said, 'If you lend me as much money as I have with me now, I'll deposit £100 with you.' The bank manager agreed and Mr Smith deposited the money.

In a third bank Mr Smith again said, 'If you lend me as much money as I have with me now, I'll deposit £100 with you.' The bank manager agreed. After this, Mr Smith had no money left.

How much money did Mr Smith have to begin with?

2 Mr Taylor, Mr Howard and Mr Miller work for the same company and have offices on the same corridor, next door to each other. Mr Taylor has the middle office. They work as marketing manager, public relations officer and accountant, but not necessarily in that order.

The marketing manager takes Mr Howard's telephone calls when he is not in the office. The accountant and Mr Miller usually have lunch together; the accountant knocks on the wall between their offices when it is time to go for lunch.

Which job does each man have?

Young Enterprise

1 Here is an extract from a pamphlet explaining what 'Young Enterprise' is.

What is 'Young Enterprise'?

Young Enterprise offers young people between the ages of 15 and 19 an exciting way of making the difficult transition from school to work.

It does this by providing prospective or recent school-leavers with the opportunity of operating a real-life industrial enterprise, a scale-model company, with real problems, real solutions, real failures and real successes.

Guess from the context the meaning of *real-life* and *scale-model*.

2 Work in pairs. Student A will read Text A; Student B will read Text B.

1 Read through all the questions.
2 Read *your* text and answer as many of the questions as you can. Note: you will not be able to answer all of them.
3 Find out from your partner the answers to the questions you have not been able to answer.

Questions

1 Where did the idea of Young Enterprise originate?
2 When did it start in the UK?
3 Is Young Enterprise part of the school curriculum?
4 How many young people are there in a typical Young Enterprise company?
5 Who decides what a Young Enterprise company will manufacture?
6 How does a Young Enterprise company raise money?
7 What is an Achiever?
8 What is an Adviser?
9 What are two essential qualifications of an Adviser?
10 What is a Sponsor?
11 Do Sponsors benefit financially from their participation in Young Enterprise?
12 Who does the company's accounting and marketing?
13 What happens to a Young Enterprise company at the end of the school year?

Text A

The scheme

In its most usual form, a Young Enterprise 'company' consists of some 20 boys and girls, either still at school or in training for a job. They all take a hand in its 'incorporation', subscribe to its Memorandum and Articles of Association (and discover the meaning of such documents), decide on the company name and on the product it will manufacture. They elect a board of management from among themselves, raise capital by selling 'shares', organise production, do market research, sell the products. They handle real money and they will have to account for the way they have managed their business.

Young Enterprise issues each of its 'companies' with the material necessary to keep records and organise business systems. The participants are advised by a team of volunteers who have experience of industry and commerce and who can guide the steps of the company's management, sharing with the young people their practical knowledge of accountancy, production management and salesmanship. But they do not instruct or direct.

At the end of the business 'year', the company will go into voluntary liquidation, and will report to the shareholders, declaring a dividend if there is a surplus.

In the process, members of the company may have to make an informed choice of career.

Young Enterprise is a part-time activity for about nine months, from autumn to early summer. Participation is entirely voluntary, quite distinct and apart from school work or vocational training.

Text B

The idea

Young Enterprise is a serious endeavour to teach all types of young people the general principles of running a business undertaking.

The idea of Young Enterprise originated in the United States of America. It was introduced into Britain by Walter Salomon, a City of London banker who formed the first National Council in 1962. After a slow start the organisation grew rapidly and the scheme is now backed by industry and commerce, so that today young people throughout the United Kingdom can participate.

A participant in Young Enterprise is known as an **Achiever**. Young Enterprise caters primarily for young people who are still at school, giving them an understanding of industry and the opportunities it may offer them in the future. But it is usually possible to include young people in the same age group who are already in a job or who have left school but have not yet started work.

An **Adviser** is a practising business executive with an expert knowledge of his own field who volunteers to help a Young Enterprise 'company' during its trading year. An ability to get on with young people and to put across the subject is of the utmost importance. As the name implies, **Advisers** are there to **advise**: they do not run the companies.

Normally, three **Advisers** are available to each company – one on accountancy, one on production and one on marketing. They may come from one organisation, or a single industry or from a variety of business occupations.

A **Sponsor** is an organisation which participates in Young Enterprise and at its own expense provides facilities by making available accommodation, advice and encouragement. **Sponsors** are rewarded only by the success of the enterprise of 'their' **Achievers**.

3

You can learn more about Young Enterprise by listening to two interviews on the cassette. As you listen do the exercises below.

Interview 1: Geoffrey Harding, former Director General, Young Enterprise

Listen and answer these questions.

1 What do Young Achievers do during the first three or four weeks after the formation of a company?
2 How long do Advisers help for?
3 What are some of the problems that Young Enterprise companies face during their operation?
4 Are these statements TRUE or FALSE?
  a The majority of companies do not suffer financial loss.
  b The average company has a turnover of a few hundred pounds.
  c The main emphasis of the Young Enterprise programme is the learning experience, not whether a company breaks even.

Interview 2: Josh Dalby and Andrew Collins, Highbury Grove Boys School, London

Josh Dalby and Andrew Collins (both aged 16) have been members of a Young Enterprise company based at their school. Their company produced attractive stationery and toiletry gift sets. The two boys were interviewed shortly after their company had gone into liquidation.

Josh was Sales and Publicity Manager. Andrew was Production Manager. Draw a table like the one below and list the main responsibilities that you think each boy must have had.

Josh: Sales and Publicity	Andrew: Production

Now listen to the interview and do the exercises below.

1 Josh explains his responsibilities as Sales and Publicity Manager. Add anything that is missing from your list above. Delete anything that you now think is wrong.

2 Josh lists the people who bought goods from the company. Look at the list below and underline the people he mentions.

teachers
girls at the neighbouring school
friends
policemen
local shopkeepers
parents
relatives
Rotary Club members

3 Josh also lists places where the goods are sold. Underline the places he mentions.

stalls at parents' evenings at school
local shops
school fetes
school jumble sales
local jumble sales
street markets

4 Andrew explains his responsibilities as Production Manager. Add anything that is missing from your list above. Delete anything that you now think is wrong.

5 First Andrew, then Josh, tell the interviewer what they feel they have learned from their experience with a Young Enterprise company. As you listen to them, put a tick (✓) in the appropriate column beside what each boy says he has learned.

Andrew	Josh	has learned
		how real business works
		how to work with others
		the importance of good communications
		how to handle people
		the jobs different people do in business
		how to behave responsibly

Find the Hidden Word

1 In pairs solve the puzzle. All the words occur in *Young Enterprise Texts A and B* on pages 63 – 4.

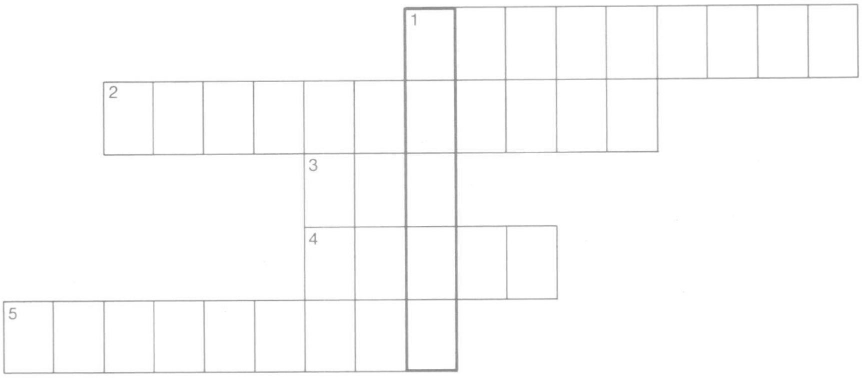

1 the theory and practice of selling
2 an owner of shares
3 Young Enterprise teaches young people how to . . . a business.
4 to choose by vote
5 At the end of the year every Young Enterprise company goes into . . . liquidation.

2 In pairs design your own *Find-the-Hidden-Word* puzzle using about 7 – 10 words that you would like to review from the listening and reading texts in this unit.

One way of designing the puzzle is to:

1 Decide what the hidden word is and write it vertically down the page. The hidden word should have 7 – 10 letters.
2 Choose the words you are going to put in the puzzle. They must each have one letter from the hidden word.
3 Write the clues, using definitions, sentence completions, pictures etc.

3 Exchange your completed puzzle with that of another pair. Solve their puzzle.

Set for Survival

However much we may enjoy our work, which one of us would not admit to bad days as well as good? And it is on these bad days that you need to be fully equipped simply to survive. With help from colleagues we've compiled an essential kit for the business person to cope with everyday office problems.

Forget the sandwiches – this is what the well-prepared business person's briefcase should contain:

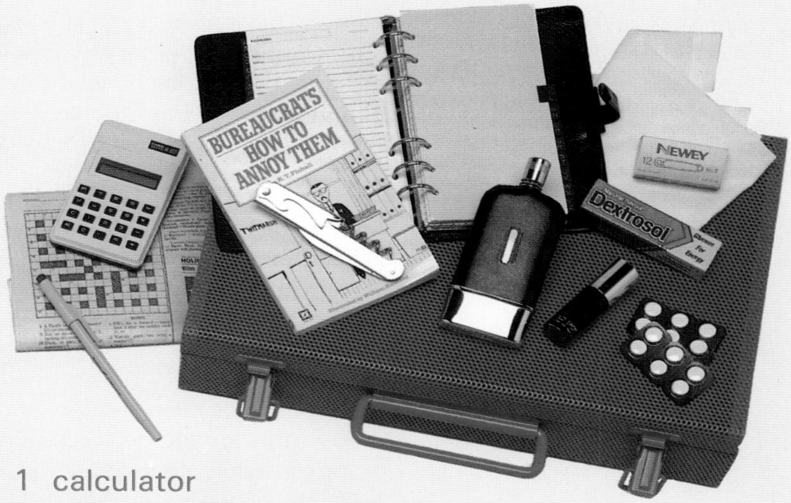

1 calculator
2 erasable ball-point pen
3 a book ***Bureaucrats, How to Annoy Them***
4 a leather ring binder
5 a penknife with bottle-opener and corkscrew
6 a hip flask
7 a large white handkerchief
8 a pack of safety pins
9 glucose tablets
10 breath-freshener
11 indigestion tablets

In pairs:
1 Look at the list of items and identify each one in the photograph.
2 For each item suggest an occasion when it would be useful in the office.
3 Compare your ideas with other students' suggestions.
4 Read the rest of the text on page 104.

Adapted from *The Observer*

The Wholesome Bread Co-operative

Adapted from *Job Ownership* (Job Ownership Ltd.)

Role-play

What is a co-operative?
A workers' co-operative is an enterprise owned and controlled by those who *work* in it. It can come into existence in two ways, either through the conversion of an already established company, or the setting up of such a co-operative from scratch.

Workers' co-operatives can offer important advantages compared with conventional businesses. One problem they may help to solve is the problem of industrial strife: battles between management and the shop floor. In a workers' co-operative where the workers are the owners and themselves appoint management such battles should occur less frequently.

Another problem is the alienation of people at work – alienation because so many have no real say in how their working lives are run. Work is controlled by big company employers, big unions and big government, and they have little chance of making their wishes felt. Many people have a longing for greater independence. Workers' co-ops may be one way of moving towards that.

The Situation
The Wholesome Bread Company, which manufactures bread, has recently become a co-operative. You are on the elected board of directors. Various suggestions and problems have arisen which must be dealt with.

The Task
1 Study the problems below and on the next page and decide what action *you* think should be taken (a, b or c). Record your answer in the appropriate column.
2 Form a group with three or four other people. You are the board of directors. Discuss each point with the group and reach a decision by consensus.

	Your decision	The Board's decision
1 It has been suggested that it is discriminatory that office workers do not have to go through the formality of clocking-in whereas shopfloor workers have to clock in and clock out. **a** Abolish clocking-in for everyone **b** Make clocking-in compulsory for everyone **c** Abolish clocking-in but make latecomers answerable to a disciplinary committee elected by the workforce		
2 According to the 'equal pay for all' policy, all workers are paid on a flat rate. It has now become almost impossible to recruit skilled workers as skilled workers can always earn more at other factories. **a** Create differentials so that skilled workers earn more than unskilled workers **b** Rotate all jobs so that each member changes his job within the factory every six months **c** Send unskilled workers on 1-year courses to train them in skilled work		

	Your decision	The Board's decision
3 Amongst the elected board there is no-one with professional management expertise or experience. **a** Appoint a salaried executive director in an advisory capacity to the co-operative **b** Send two members on short management courses **c** Make everyone on the board responsible for reading up and becoming acquainted with general management principles and issues		
4 Mass meetings have to be held before any major policy decisions can be made. These are at present unpaid. Complaints have been received that these meetings are taking up too much of the members' leisure hours. **a** Halt production lines an hour early when meetings are to be held **b** Pay members the usual hourly rate when they are attending meetings outside hours **c** Members should accept these meetings as a necessary part of belonging to a co-operative		
5 The question of distribution of profits has arisen. **a** Reinvest most of the profits in the company for general expansion **b** Share most of the profits equally between all members at the end of the financial year **c** Use most of the profits to improve social and environmental conditions within the factory, e.g. providing a crèche, social evenings, etc.		
6 The question of whether members should retain their trade union membership has arisen. **a** This should be left up to the individual **b** There should be compulsory membership for all members of the co-operative **c** Union membership is not recommended as the co-operative itself is committed to protecting the members' interests		
7 Some new members have been criticized as being destructive elements. It has been suggested that not all workers be members of the co-operative. **a** Workers can join the co-operative after a six-month trial period **b** All workers should automatically be members immediately they join the workforce **c** Workers may only become members after being voted in		

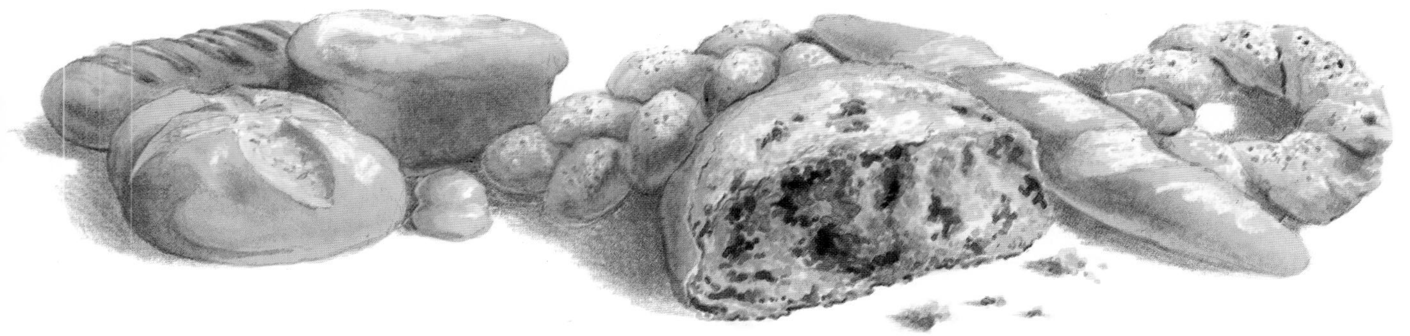

8 ▸▸ *Advertising*

The Advertising Standards Authority

The text below gives information about the British Advertising Standards Authority. Read it and answer these questions:

1 What is the aim of the Advertising Standards Authority?
2 How does the Advertising Standards Authority find out about unacceptable advertisements?
3 Look at the advertisements on the next page. Would they all be accepted by the Advertising Standards Authority?
4 Find these expressions in the text and guess their meaning:

flexing our muscles
flowery prose
to pull something out by the roots
to show someone the door
a yardstick
to breach the rules
to bend the rules

DO ADVERTISEMENTS SOMETIMES DISTORT THE TRUTH?

The short answer is yes, some do.

Every week hundreds of thousands of advertisements appear for the very first time.

Nearly all of them play fair with the people they are addressed to.

A handful do not. They misrepresent the products they are advertising.

As the Advertising Standards Authority it is our job to make sure these ads are identified, and stopped.

WHAT MAKES AN ADVERTISEMENT MISLEADING?

If a training course had turned a 7 stone weakling into Mr Universe the fact could be advertised because it can be proved.

But a promise to build 'you' into a 15 stone he-man would have us flexing our muscles because the promise could not always be kept.

'Makes you look younger' might be a reasonable claim for a cosmetic.

But pledging to 'take years off your life' would be an overclaim akin to a promise of eternal youth.

A garden centre's claim that its seedlings would produce 'a riot of colour in just a few days' might be quite contrary to the reality.

Such flowery prose would deserve to be pulled out by the roots.

If a brochure advertised a hotel as being '5 minutes walk to the beach', it must not require an Olympic athlete to do it in the time.

As for estate agents, if the phrase 'overlooking the river' translated to 'backing onto a ditch', there would be nothing for it but to show their ad the door.

HOW DO WE JUDGE THE ADS WE LOOK INTO?

Our yardstick is The British Code of Advertising Practice.

Its 500 rules give advertisers precise practical guidance on what they can and cannot say.

WHY IT'S A TWO-WAY PROCESS

Unfortunately some advertisers are unaware of the Code, and breach the rules unwittingly. Others forget, bend or deliberately ignore the rules.

That is why we keep a continuous check on advertising. But because of the sheer volume, we cannot monitor every advertiser all the time.

So we encourage the public to help by telling us about any advertisements they think ought not to have appeared. Last year over 7,500 people wrote to us.

The Advertising Standards Authority. ✓
If an advertisement is wrong, we're here to put it right.

ASA Ltd, Dept. T, Brook House, Torrington Place, London WC1E 7HN.

Here's how much sugar the average woman consumes in a lifetime.
Here's how to consume only a quarter of it.
The average British woman consumes 1.22 tons of sugar during the course of her lifetime.
Sucron looks like sugar, tastes like sugar, sprinkles like sugar and like sugar, you can cook with it.
Yet because it's four times sweeter than sugar, you use only a quarter as much.
What would you rather use?
sucron

A BIRDS EYE VIEW OF MAKING ENDS MEAT.
We've all got the problem.
Balancing our diet and balancing our budget. That's why most of us regard a really good piece of meat as strictly a week-end luxury.
But take the Birds Eye View and your perspective can change. We've created a top quality, man-sized meal at a price we can all afford seven days a week.
It's called Steakhouse Grills.
Tender flakes of juicy beef– with no gristle. Just delicately seasoned to be equally tasty rare, medium or well-done.
Now, we're the first to admit it isn't a traditional steak. But, once you've tried it, we're sure you'll admit it's a delicious alternative.
So why not take the Birds Eye View? It always looks much nicer.
BIRDS EYE
STEAKHOUSE
2 BEEF GRILLS
G OUT FOR YOU.

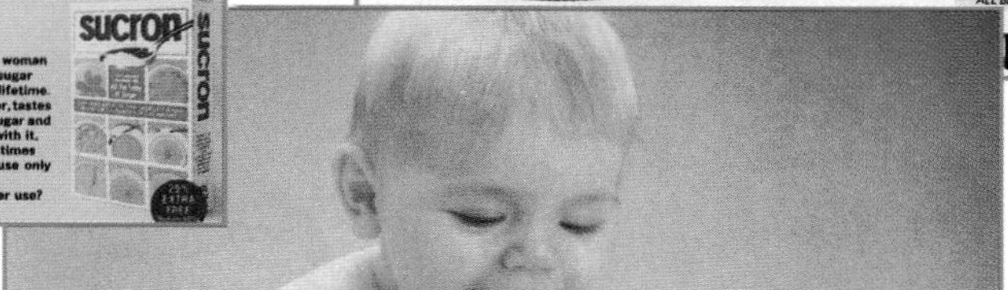
He's researching surface texture, differentiating between colours, and developing his audio-sensory perception.
He thinks he's playing with a rattle.
When every waking moment of your child's play is spent learning, his toys should also play a part.
DUPLO Baby Toys are made in bright colours, have funny faces, and make unexpected little squeaks and rattles to keep him playing happily. But while they're doing this, they're also busy developing and improving his co-ordination.
The pieces are just the right size for little hands. With rounded edges so they're safe for little fingers.
What's more, as your child grows and develops, so do the toys.
duplo

THE PERSONAL COMPUTER FAMILY WITH EUROPEAN KNOW-HOW
RIENDLY & COMPATIBLE

At Scandinavian World you can see the wood from the trees

Johnnie Walker
BLACK LABEL
OTHER PRESENTS PALE BESIDE IT

Advertising Features

1 There are many different ways in which advertisements in magazines catch our attention.

Look at the list of advertising features below. Can you think of any more to add to the list?

* Use of the word *natural*
* Use of the word *right*
* Exaggeration, e.g. *the best . . ., the most . . .*
* Promises
* Commanding you
* Offering you a whole lifestyle behind the product
* Using a 'scientific' image
* Playing on guilt, fear, inadequacy
* Appealing to snobbery
* Using puns and catch phrases
* Featuring animals
* Featuring children
* Featuring the countryside
* Suggestive, using sexual imagery
* Traditional, the 'good old days'
* Fantasy
* Suggesting you'll be a social (especially sexual) success
*
*
*

From *Getting Started* (Workers Educational Association)

2 In small groups look at the advertisements on the previous page and any other adverts that are available.

Identify which of the features in the list above are present in each of the advertisements.

3 What would happen if there was no advertising? Do you think products should be sold – and could be sold – simply on their own merit?

Drive an Ad!

1 How would you like to drive around inside an ad for KP Nuts, Levi jeans or Cadbury chocolates?

The marketing company responsible for these advertisements is Poster Motors, one of the Dun and Bradstreet Group, based in London. Their method is simple: a fleet of car owners is recruited, their cars are all sprayed in the same base colour, decorated in the livery of the advertiser – and off they go! For the advertiser it is a straight branding exercise. But why does a car owner do it? Is it a way of making money? Of attracting attention?

What do you think? In pairs, try to *guess* the answers to the quiz.

QUIZ

1 Poster Motors uses
   (a) Volkswagen 'Beetles' and British Leyland Morris 'Minis'
   (b) any car, from Rolls Royces to 'Minis'
   (c) only 'Minis'

2 Poster Motors drivers are paid
   (a) £6 a month
   (b) £16 a month
   (c) £60 a month

3 Morris 'Minis' are used because
   (a) all classes of people drive them
   (b) mostly young people drive them
   (c) the 'Mini' is the most popular car in Britain

4 Poster Motors drivers are
   (a) usually under 35 years of age
   (b) often middle-aged and unmarried
   (c) all ages – teenagers to grannies

5 Poster Motors drivers are usually
   (a) introverts
   (b) extroverts
   (c) in need of money

6 Poster Motors operates
   (a) only in Britain
   (b) in Britain and Ireland
   (c) all over Europe

From *Business Express* (Modern English Publications)

2 On the cassette you can hear an interview with David Barnes, the Sales Director of Poster Motors. Listen and check how many answers you got right in the quiz.

It Pays to Advertise

1 Read the rhyme. Notice that in the first three couplets, a contrast is made between the codfish and the hen. This will help you *guess* the meaning of the underlined words – if you don't know the meaning already!

The codfish lays a million eggs,
The helpful hen lays one.

The codfish makes no fuss of its achievement,
The hen boasts what she's done.

We forget the gentle codfish,
The hen we eulogise;

Which teaches us this lesson that –
It pays to advertise.

Anon.

From *The Faber Book of Useful Verse*

2 Listen to the rhyme being read aloud on the cassette.

3 Practise reciting the rhyme yourself, paying particular attention to rhythm.

Song of the Open Road

From *I Wouldn't Have Missed It – Selected Poems of Ogden Nash* (André Deutsch)

Read the poem. What is the poet complaining about?

I think that I shall never see
A billboard lovely as a tree.*
Indeed, unless the billboards fall
I'll never see a tree at all.
Ogden Nash

* *a billboard* is a large board used for displaying advertisements. *Billboard* is an American English word. In British English *boarding* is more common.

Freedom in a Pie

1 What is your reaction to the pie in this advertisement? Does it:

look sickly sweet?
make your mouth water?
leave you cold?

Using language that makes it quite clear what your reaction is, describe the pastry and the filling, as well as the pie as a whole.

2 Read the first two paragraphs of Noel Radcliffe's article 'Freedom in a Pie'.

I once bought a big firm's pie because the picture on the carton was a real gem of colour printing and showed a fine photograph of an apricot pie. Part of the pastry had been cut away, making a great crusty maw out of which a strong build-up of apricots, carried on a torrent of glistening thick syrup, spilled out in eager display.

From the carton I slid out a geometrically exact pie, somehow lacking the glow of promise in that picture, and cut it open. In my mouth the masticatory juices compelled by the picture were already beginning to retreat. On the floor of a great empty cavern of nothing, lay one-eighth of an inch of 'jam'. I had been well and truly conned. Instinctively I dropped the knife and reached for my pen, and wrote: 'Dear Sirs, Herewith is a packet cover which contains a half (or less) truth . . . The half (or more) untruth is the great gush of apricot filling. . . . I regard this as being a serious deception, especially as the picture appears to be a photograph of the real thing. Yours, etc., N. Ratcliffe.'

1 What was the author's reaction to the pie in the picture?
2 What was his reaction to the pie itself?
3 Guess the meaning of *conned*.

3

Look at the paragraphs again and notice the kind of language the writer uses. Find examples of:

'flowery' language
exaggeration
stiff, formal language

4

Paragraphs 3–9 quote from seven more letters, all concerning the pie and the picture on the packet. Read the paragraphs and use the table below to:

1 Note down who wrote each letter.
2 Describe the purpose of each letter by choosing one (or two) phrases from the list below.

to apologize
to make a complaint
to request further information
to put forward a defence
to express indignation
to describe action that has been taken
to give further information

Letters	to	from	Purpose
Paragraph 3	the author		
Paragraph 4	the pie manufacturers		
Paragraph 5	the author		
Paragraph 6	District Inspector, Weights & Measures Office		
Paragraph 7	the author		
Paragraph 8	Peter Jackson, MP		
Paragraph 9	Peter Jackson, MP		

Came the reply: Dear Madam [apparently only a woman can have opinions on pies], . . . We are very sorry indeed that you should have received a pie that did not come up to our usual high standard. It would seem a slight fault has occurred with the filling machine and we regret that the operator did not notice that the pie had been filled incorrectly.

'. . . We are attaching a postal order . . . We hope you will use this to buy another of our products which we feel sure will give you entire satisfaction.'

Some time later I bought and opened another apricot pie. Then I wrote again: 'Dear Sirs . . . I think I may assume that though two of your thousands of pies might be filled incorrectly, it is hardly likely that the two would pick on the same person. The second pie is not better than the first. The contrast between what appears to be a colour photograph of an opened pie and the actual thing inside is so marked as to be ludicrous, and has all the appearance of gross and cynical misrepresentation. I am sending a copy of this letter to my MP. . .

'Dear Sir [so man *can* have an opinion on pies], . . . some of the sweeping accusations . . . compel me to reaffirm our principles and intentions. You have used such phrases as "serious deception" "ludicrous contrast" . . . If all these expressions added up to a reasonable description of our business it would be suprising that we have survived for over 130 years . . . and retained an extremely high reputation. The illustrations on our cartons are photographic artists' representations. Obviously, as befits his task, the artist will "dress up" his model to make the most attractive photograph . . . the filling used is not jam . . . we use a properly-made pie filling . . . the quantity involved is originally determined by our development technologists and is related to the amount of pastry . . . to produce the best possible ''eat''.'

Some time later I bought yet another of the pies. There was still that gaping gap. But in the meantime the *Trade Description Act* had been passed.

'District Inspector, Weights and Measures Office – Dear Sir, Making the, to my mind, rational asumption that illustrations can misrepresent just as much as words . . . it strikes me that consideration might well be given to the shockingly exaggerated pictorial representations on some containers of their contents. I have in mind, as an example, the cartons containing ''fruit'' pies (see enclosure). On the cover you will notice . . .'

'Dear Mr Ratcliffe, Inquiries have already been commenced . . . I am wondering if you would let me have copies of these letters (referred to). Undoubtedly I shall be writing to the Company in due course and it might be useful to know exactly how they reacted to your own complaint. Chief Inspector, Weights and Measures Dept.

'From Weights and Measures Dept. to Peter M. Jackson, MP. Dear Sir, . . . I can inform you that active steps are being taken by the Company to obtain new supplies of cartons which will be altered in design so as not to offend against the provisions of the *Trade Description Act, 1968*. . . . other steps are being taken to . . . obliteration of the picture on the carton. I might mention that the pulp is fed through a fairly small orifice, having been initially crushed . . . therefore the fill cannot have the appearance of fruit in its true form. Chief Inspector.'

'From the Parliamentary Secretary, Board of Trade. Dear Peter (Jackson), . . . The relevant sections of the Act define ''trade description'' as an indication, direct or indirect and *by whatever means given*, of a number of physical characteristics . . . I have no doubt in my mind that a trade description can be applied to goods by means of a pictorial representation of those goods. Sincerely, Gwyneth Dunwoody.'

5

Now read paragraphs 10 and 11. Did the author's attempt to right a wrong succeed?

On the cartons of small fruit pies made by the firm in question, a silver rectangle now obliterates that tasty-looking avalanche of fruit. Except the one I bought the other day. Same seductive picture. Same unseductive cavity. (Our pie cavities are non-fattening.) I tipped the pie up on my plate. Yes, a trickle of the stuff did actually move. It was an improvement on that rigid one-eighth of an inch of 'jam'.

I thought of that first 'It would seem a slight fault has occurred with the filling machine.' Then the 'Obviously, as befits his task, the artist ''dolls up'' his model.' Then 'steps are being taken' to obliterate the picture. To adapt Blake:

Hold eternity of procedure in the hollow of a crust,
And Freedom in a Pie.

Noel Radcliffe

6

In line 64 *that tasty avalanche of fruit* refers to the picture. Find a phrase in the same paragraph that refers to the real pie.

7

In line 65 *cavity* describes the hole where the pie filling is. Look back over the article and find other words and phrases used to describe this hole.

8

In line 70 *dolls up* is not an exact quotation. Find the original reference. What is the difference in meaning?

9

In the last paragraph the author refers to a poem by William Blake *Auguries of Innocence*. The original lines referred to are from the beginning of the poem:

To see a World in a Grain of Sand
And Heaven in a Wild Flower,
Hold Infinity in the palm of your hand
And Eternity in an hour.

What do Blake's lines mean? What does the author's adaptation of these lines mean?

10

When words commonly occur together we say they 'collocate', e.g. *sweeping accusations* (line 27), *a high reputation* (line 33). What are some common collocations of these words?

a torrent	a cavity	crusty
a trickle	a maw	seductive
a cavern	an avalanche	rigid

11

What is the meaning of these expressions?

to pick on (line 22)
to cut away (line 3)
to cut open (line 6)

Use a monolingual dictionary to find other expressions with *to pick* and *to cut*. Write some sentences that illustrate some of the expressions you have found and that you wish to remember. Leave a blank where the expression should be. Ask other students to complete your sentences.

Describe and Draw

Work in pairs.

Player A
Describe one of the pictures on page 79 to Player B. Do not show the picture to B.

Player B
Draw the picture as accurately as possible. You may ask A any questions you wish about the picture. When you have finished, compare your drawing with A's picture.

Repeat the game with Player B describing one of the pictures on page 101 to Player A.

Commad Ltd.

Role-play

The Situation

Commad Ltd. is a small advertising company that specializes in producing commercials for local radio and TV stations. It has been asked to produce sufficient commercials to fill a five-minute transmission slot. The commercials are for companies whose magazine advertisements appear on page 71.

Roles

Production manager

As head of the production team, your task is to:

1 make sure that the commercials are recorded and ready for playback within the period of time you have available.

2 ask your team to work in small groups, each group working on one commercial.

3 look carefully at all the magazine advertisements on page 71 with all the members of the production team and decide which advertisements they are going to work on.

4 make sure that each group knows how much time they have. You have a five-minute commercial slot to fill, at peak hours (19.30 – 21.00 hours). You should not over-run, but you can run under five minutes.

Members of the production team

Your task is to:

1 produce five minutes of commercials, to be transmitted at peak hours (19.30 – 21.00 hours).

2 look carefully at all the magazine advertisements on page 71 and decide which advertisements you wish to work on to make commercials.

3 keep to the deadlines given you by the Production Manager.

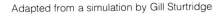

Adapted from a simulation by Gill Sturtridge

Describe and draw

Pictures for Player A.

9 Sex and gender

A Riddle

Can you solve this riddle?

> A man and his son are driving along. They have a bad accident. The boy is taken to hospital. The surgeon comes out of the operating theatre, looks at the boy and says 'Oh, my God. It's my own son!'
>
> Explain the surgeon's response.

Explain why you found the riddle difficult to solve. (If you didn't find it difficult, explain why some other people might find it difficult!)

What Has Sex Got to Do With It?

1 Read the text and answer the questions.

> When linguists approach the topic of sex – in their books, at any rate – they do something which at first sight seems very strange. They don't usually refer to 'sex' at all. Instead, they talk about 'gender'. 'Masculine' and 'feminine' genders, for instance. Nouns, adjectives and often other parts of speech are said to be masculine, or feminine, and often 'neuter' as well.
>
> There's nothing prudish about this. There's a good reason why you have to talk about 'gender' rather than 'sex' when you're looking at a language. It's because the genders that turn up in a language don't necessarily have anything to do with sex at all. Words that are 'masculine gender' often don't refer to male beings. 'Feminine gender' words are often not female.
>
> For instance, if you were learning French, one of the first things you'd notice is the way that all nouns in the language fall into one of two types. When you want to say '*the* something-or-other', you find that there are thousands of words which go with *le*, and thousands more which go with *la*.
> *Le* words include:
> *le fromage* 'cheese' *le sexe* 'sex'
> *La* words include:
> *la pomme* 'apple' *la poche* 'pocket'

You've got to get it right, if you want your French to be acceptable. *Le pomme* sounds awful to a Frenchman.

In English, fortunately, things are a lot simpler! There's no gender as there is in French. *The* stays *the*, and it can be used with almost every noun in the language. It wasn't always like this. In Anglo-Saxon times, there were genders similar to those used in German – and several forms of the word *the*, for instance. But these days, gender has all but disappeared; the only way you could group nouns into gender types today is by seeing how they pattern in relation to such pronouns as *he*, *she* and *it*. And when you sort them out like this, you find that the types are pretty logical. In English, gender and sex do go very well together. They make a lovely couple.

From *Who Cares about English Usage?* by David Crystal (Pelican)

1 What is meant by the grammatical term 'gender'?
2 What is the relation between gender and sex (a) in French and (b) in English?
3 Does your language have 'masculine' and 'feminine' genders?
4 What other languages do you know of where gender is an important aspect of the grammatical system?

2

As David Crystal implies in the text above, most nouns in English don't show gender. However, a few English words show gender in their endings. Complete this table:

masculine	feminine
actor	....
host	....
waiter	....
hero	....
....	widow
....	bride
policeman	....

3

With some words it is not possible to tell whether they are 'male' or 'female'. One example is *cousin*. The ambiguity can cause surprises. Imagine situations in which these might be said:

'You didn't tell me your cousin was a girl!'
'I wasn't expecting you to bring your *boy* friend.'
'It's a woman driver.'

4

What gender are these words usually presumed to be?

doctor surgeon engineer nurse secretary chairman

5

On the cassette you can hear a radio talk by David Crystal, on another aspect of English gender.

Before you listen, complete the following sentences with what you feel are the most appropriate pronouns.

1 England is proud of . . . . . history.
2 A stamp collector looking at one of his stamps: 'Isn't . . . . . beautiful?'
3 A car owner, talking about his car: '. . . . . handles superbly.'

4 A parent: 'The baby again – always crying! Will . . . . . never stop?'
5 A host to his guests: 'Anyone can have a drink if . . . . . want(s).'

As you listen, do the following:

1 Check the pronouns you chose in the sentences above with those that David Crystal says are most likely to be used.
2 What other examples does he give of unusual pronoun use? What is the effect?
3 List the alternatives that have been suggested to replace *he* after *someone*, *anyone*. Which alternative is likely to survive in the long term?

6 Look up *gender* in a grammar book (e.g. *Practical English Usage* by Michael Swan, OUP). Compare how the points that David Crystal has made in his talk are dealt with in the grammar book.

Sex Stereotyping

From *The Gender Trap*, Book 1, by C Adams and R Laurikietis (Virago in association with Quartet Books)

1 Discuss this statement.

> Almost from the moment you are born you are taught how to be a male, or how to be a female . . . You were taught the difference in all sorts of ways; some are obvious and hard to miss, others are not so obvious. But you were taught nevertheless that being a boy is one thing, being a girl another. This is what is meant by sex-role stereotyping.

You may wish to consider the following questions:

1 How do parents dress small boys and small girls, from babyhood on?
2 What toys are boys and girls given? What games and activities are they encouraged to take part in?
3 Do adults use different language for boys and girls?
4 Does school education differ for boys and girls?
5 Is it possible to avoid sex-stereotyping?

2 Below are some words and phrases often used in connection with children. Which of them do you think are used most often about a boy, and which about a girl?

Boys will be boys	How sweet!	A tomboy
A little devil	A good sport	Sensitive
Bossy	A little angel	Aren't you adorable!
As pretty as a picture	A cry-baby	

3 How would you like to change sex for the day?

1 Take 5–7 minutes to think about how you would spend the day as a member of the opposite sex. Make notes about what you would do and how your habits and personality would be affected.
2 In small groups describe your day to each other. Judging from these accounts, who does the group seem to feel has more fun: men or women?

Working in a Night-Club

1 This waitress works in a fashionable night club in London. What do you think it would be like to do her job? Discuss some of the advantages and disadvantages. What forms of sexism is a woman in this job likely to experience?

2 Below is an article that appeared on the Woman's Page of *The Guardian*. Read the first two paragraphs. What is the article about?

ON A busy night Graham Flander has his bottom slapped 30 times. Men pinch him as he walks by and say, "Hello, darling, what are you doing afterwards?" Or they wonder what a nice girl like him is doing in a place like this.

These are everyday aggravations for many women but they are not the sort of remarks that men are used to receiving. But then, not many men earn their living as Graham Flander does. This 20-year-old son of a Portsmouth security man works as a waitress at The Hippodrome, London's latest mega-discotheque.

The job has given him a unique insight into female experience. Nightclub waitresses are hired for their looks. They must smile prettily, serve drinks and ingratiate themselves to the men who pay the bills and leave them handsome tips. A more perfectly sexist situation it would be hard to imagine.

'I don't blame girls for not liking being harassed at work. I get it all the time.'

"I've got a lot more sympathy for women since I started working here," says Graham. "Feminists hate the patronising way that men treat them. I think some of them are extremists, but a lot of it is true. I don't blame girls for not liking being harassed at work. I get it all the time. You have to get used to it. You learn things to say. You laught it off."

Graham has been in this extraordinary position since the night he and some friends – all dressed with fashionable androgyny – turned up to a party night at the club. He asked one of the staff if there were any jobs going – for a man – and the request was passed on to the Hippodrome's owner, Peter Stringfellow.

Stringfellow, who has a taste for the profitably bizarre, said he could only give him a job as a waitress. It was not a possibility that had occurred to Graham, but he accepted for the same reasons as any girl just up from the provinces; the job was glamorous, well-paid and offered the chance to meet famous people. Clearly he has unusual predilections, but he says he is not a transvestite, simply – *a la* Boy George – a man who chooses to dress in clothes not conventionally thought of as male, just as a woman might choose to wear a mannish look.

"He's not there as a freak," Stringfellow remarks. "He just happens to look like a very beautiful woman. I consider him as a friend. I'm hoping to push society into greater gentleness and tolerance."

So, five nights a week for the past four months, Graham has turned up for work in his jeans, gone upstairs to the ladies' changing room and spent two hours transforming himself into an approximation of womanhood. A blonde wig and two-inch fingernails and a lot of make-up are followed by a pink leotard and tutu, stockings, suspenders and stiletto heels.

'It's just people rather than a man and seven girls.'

The real girls in the room seem to have become used to his presence; "The first time I walked into the changing room it went very quiet and I got a few looks. Now it's fine. I go up there to get dressed and I chat to the girls. I'm Graham and they're Nanette and Julie and so on. It's just people rather than a man and seven girls."

The public, however, are not to know that once Graham gets down to the business of serving drinks. As he says: "People see my long hair and my outfit and they assume that I'm female. I get chatted up an awful lot. If I speak they know I'm a man, but you can get away with just smiling and laughing. If men see a blonde they don't expect any intelligence."

That is one of the lessons that girls learn just by growing up, but Graham has chosen to take a crash course in the compromises and accommodations that are made when men become the opposition: "You start thinking of men as a separate sex and treating them as women do," he says. "You learn when to laugh, when not to. You have to be more modest if you're a girl. You tend to let men hold the conversation and you just return it. You give opinions, but you don't hold them too strongly – you tend to take second place to a degree."

Then there are the occasional outbursts of violence. "A guy walked past one time and he slapped my arse really hard. I asked him to stop so he did it again. It gets to the point where it's sadistic and not done for fun.

"But I don't want to sound as though I hate men because you also get treated nicer if you're a girl. If you're a man they slap you on the back and say, 'Allo mate.' But if you're a girl they're more gentle and give you compliments.

"Men will tell me I look sexy or georgeous. If I look like a girl I like it, but I'd hate it if they said that when I was dressed normally. People say: 'Why don't you have an operation?' But that's not the reason I'm doing this. Underneath it all I'm still a man and I don't feel like a woman even if I'm treated like one by the customers."

So he says, but there are clearly times when distinctions can become blurred: "We'll be in the changing room for an hour after work chatting about tips and the girls' boyfriends. It's girls' talk, things like, 'Oh my God, did you get the creep on the corner table?' I have the same experiences they do, so we talk about the same things. If I was working behind the bar with the guys I'd say, 'Did you see the gorgeous number in the mini?' but it seems strange telling the girls that, so if an attractive man has walked in we'll talk about that.

'It's almost like being two people instead of one. I sometimes lose track.'

"The problem is that I'll go downstairs to a situation where I've got to be a man and it can be very hard to adjust the way I think and act. It's almost like being two people instead of one. I sometimes lose track."

In the end, however, reality always intrudes. Once men know that Graham is a fellow man they tip him less well than they do the girls. After all, there's nothing in it for them: "If they flirt with a girl they think that she might say 'Yes' and go home with them. If they flirt with me they know that's all they're going to get."

And he knows that the means of escape of which the other girls in the club dream – a visiting film producer or rich husband – are closed to him. He pays the same penalties they do, but without hope of a payoff. "As soon as I can't carry this off I'll stop," he says. "At 35 I'll be wearing classic male clothes and I'll have short hair. I don't want to look like mutton dressed as lamb."

'That's the only time I've wished I was a girl.'

He says he is happy, but he must sense that he is trapped in a sort of limbo. "Two squaddies came in one night and one of them took a shine to me. He was really nice and I didn't tell him the truth because I didn't want him to be nasty to me.

"They came back a couple of times, and on the third night his mate clicked and told him. He cut me dead from then on and it really hurt because he'd have talked to me if I hadn't been a guy. That's the only time I've wished I was a girl."

Every night before the club opens Graham Flander plays his favourite song on the jukebox – Marilyn Monroe singing I Just Want To Be Loved By You from Some Like It Hot. You may recall a line of Jack Lemmon's from that film; "I tell you," he says to Tony Curtis as a real woman walks past the two stars, who are in drag, "It's a whole different sex."

Some time later Lemmon is talking to himself; "I'm a girl," he says. "I'm a girl. I'm a girl. I'm a girl . . ."

David Thomas

3 In paragraph 4 Graham Flander is quoted as saying, 'I've got a lot more sympathy for women since I started to work here.' Make a list of the experiences that Graham has had that have made him more sympathetic to women.

4 What is the attitude of the author of the article to Graham Flander and his job? What is your attitude?

5 Describe ways in which some customers may harass or patronize or flirt with the waitresses.

6 Describe ways in which the waitresses may ingratiate themselves to the customers.

7 Describe some situations in which you might:

cut someone dead
laugh something off
chat someone up
carry something off well
get away with something

8 Use a monolingual dictionary to find other examples of the pattern *to cut + adjective*. Make sentences to illustrate the meaning of two or three that you want to remember.

9 Who might say the following, in what circumstances?

'What a creep!'
'What a gorgeous number!'
'I've taken a shine to him.'

The Gift Game

1 The game is for four players. Each player must buy a gift suitable for each of the four family and friends described at his/her START square.
2 Each player has five coloured tokens. Place your tokens beside your START square.
3 Use one of your tokens to move around the board according to the throw of a dice, and following the instructions in your START square.

Player 1 Find gifts for:
the player on your left
a small girl, aged 7
someone you dislike intensely
your youngest sister, who is getting married next week

Player 4 Find gifts for:
a teenage girl
your elderly aunt, who lives alone in the country
someone who has just started a new job
your best friend

Adapted from *Communication Games* by Byrne and Rixon (NFER/Nelson/British Council)

4 If you land on a square containing a gift that you think is suitable for one of your family and friends, tell the other players why that gift is suitable and justify your choice. If they do not accept your reasons you may not buy that gift. When you have successfully bought a gift, place one of your coloured tokens on that gift square. This gift may no longer be bought by other players. *The first player to successfully buy gifts for all his family and friends is the winner of the game.*

Player 2 Find gifts for:
a teenage boy
someone you do not see very often
someone who is very depressed at the moment
your bachelor uncle who loves cooking

Player 3 Find gifts for:
a small boy, aged 4
someone you have not seen for years
someone who always gives you unusual presents
your cousin, who is crazy about sports

10 ▸▸ *A taste of literature*

Thinking about Reading

Some books are to be tasted,
others to be swallowed, and some
few to be chewed and digested.

Sir Francis Bacon (1561 – 1626)

What does this quotation mean?

Give examples of books that you have 'tasted', 'swallowed' or 'chewed and digested'.

What kind of reading material do you read for pleasure?

Have you read any English novels or short stories that you would like to recommend to other students in the class?

Do you enjoy reading 'the book of the film'?

What English or American films or TV serials have you seen that are 'the film of the book'?

The Collector

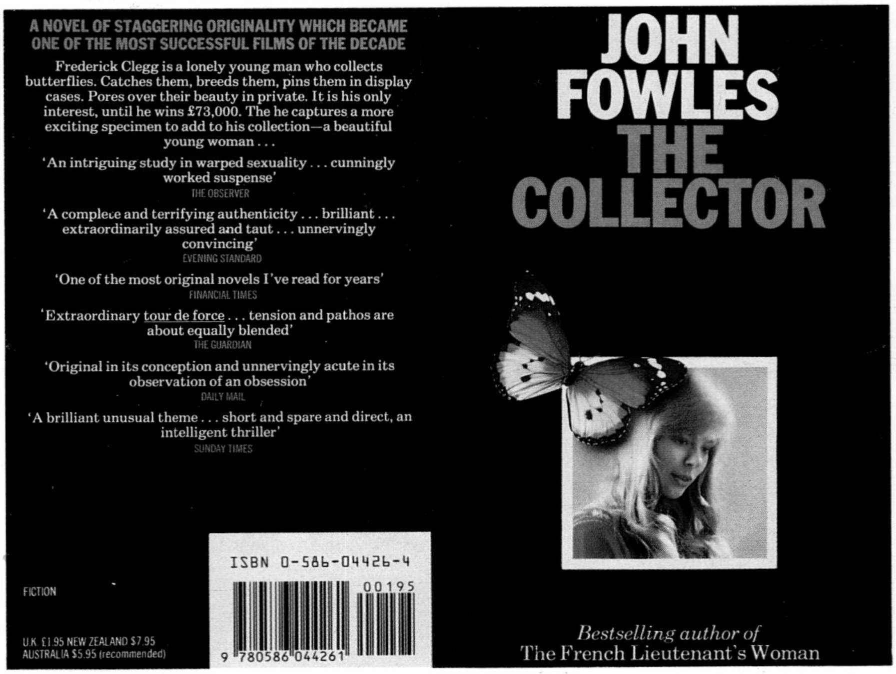

A NOVEL OF STAGGERING ORIGINALITY WHICH BECAME ONE OF THE MOST SUCCESSFUL FILMS OF THE DECADE
Frederick Clegg is a lonely young man who collects butterflies. Catches them, breeds them, pins them in display cases. Pores over their beauty in private. It is his only interest, until he wins £73,000. The he captures a more exciting specimen to add to his collection—a beautiful young woman . . .
'An intriguing study in warped sexuality . . . cunningly worked suspense'
THE OBSERVER
'A complece and terrifying authenticity . . . brilliant . . . extraordinarily assured and taut . . . unnervingly convincing'
EVENING STANDARD
'One of the most original novels I've read for years'
FINANCIAL TIMES
'Extraordinary tour de force . . . tension and pathos are about equally blended'
THE GUARDIAN
'Original in its conception and unnervingly acute in its observation of an obsession'
DAILY MAIL
'A brilliant unusual theme . . . short and spare and direct, an intelligent thriller'
SUNDAY TIMES
FICTION
U.K. £1.95 NEW ZEALAND $7.95
AUSTRALIA $5.95 (recommended)
ISBN 0-586-04426-4
JOHN FOWLES
THE COLLECTOR
Bestselling author of
The French Lieutenant's Woman

The Collector is a novel by John Fowles which was made into a film in 1969, starring Terence Stamp. A number of Fowles' other novels have been filmed, most recently *The French Lieutenant's Woman*.

1 On the previous page is the outside cover of *The Collector*. Skim read the comments about the book. (Do not worry about understanding every word.) Do you think you would enjoy reading the book? Why?/Why not?

2 The first part of *The Collector* is told from Frederick's point of view. The second part is the young woman's diary, which she kept while imprisoned. Her name is Miranda. She is an art student.

Extract 1, from the first part of the book, describes the capture of Miranda.

> Two old women with umbrellas (it began to spot with rain again) appeared and came up the road towards me. It was just what I didn't want, I knew she was due, and I nearly gave up then and there. But I bent right down, they passed talking nineteen to the dozen, I don't think they even saw me or the van. There were cars parked everywhere in that district. A minute passed. I got out and opened the back. It was all planned. And then she was near. She'd come up and round without me seeing, only twenty yards away, walking quickly. If it had been a clear night I don't know what I'd have done. But there was this wind in the trees. Gusty. I could see there was no one behind her. Then she was right beside me, coming up the pavement. Funny, singing to herself.
>
> I said, excuse me, do you know anything about dogs?
>
> She stopped, surprised. 'Why?' she said.
>
> It's awful, I've just run one over, I said. It dashed out. I don't know what to do with it. It's not dead. I looked into the back, very worried.
>
> 'Oh the poor thing,' she said.
>
> She came towards me, to look in. Just as I hoped.
>
> There's no blood, I said, but it can't move.
>
> Then she came round the end of the open back door, and I stood back as if to let her see. She bent forward to peer in, I flashed a look down the road, no one, and then I got her. She didn't make a sound, she seemed so surprised, I got the pad I'd been holding in my pocket right across her mouth and nose, I caught her to me, I could smell the fumes, she struggled like the dickens, but she wasn't strong, smaller even than I'd thought. She made a sort of gurgling. I looked down the road again, I was thinking this is it, she'll fight and I shall have to hurt her or run away. I was ready to bolt for it. And then suddenly she went limp, I was holding her up instead of holding her quiet. I got her half into the van, then I jerked open the other door, got in and pulled her in after me, then shut the doors quietly to. I rolled and lifted her on to the bed. She was mine, I felt suddenly very excited, I knew I'd done it.

Extract 2 is from Miranda's diary, written about two weeks after her capture.

October 20th

It's eleven o'clock in the morning.

I've just tried to escape.

What I did was to wait for him to unbolt the door, which opens outwards. Then to push it back as violently as possible. It's only metal-lined on this side, it's made of wood, but it's very heavy. I thought I might hit him with it and knock him out, if I did it at just the right moment.

So as soon as it began to move back, I gave it the biggest push I could manage. It knocked him back and I rushed out, but of course it depended on his being stunned. And he wasn't at all. He must have taken the force of it on his shoulder, it doesn't swing very smoothly.

At any rate he caught my jumper. For a second there was that other side of him I sense, the violence, hatred, absolute determination not to let me go. So I said, all right, and pulled myself away and went back.

He said, you might have hurt me, that door's very heavy.

I said, every second you keep me here, you hurt me.

I thought pacifists didn't believe in hurting people, he said.

I just shrugged and lit a cigarette. I was trembling.

He did all the usual morning routine in silence. Once he rubbed his shoulder in rather an obvious way. And that was that.

Now I'm going to look properly for loose stones. The tunnel idea. Of course I've looked before, but not really closely, literally stone by stone, from top to bottom of each wall.

It's evening. He's just gone away. He brought me my food. But he's been very silent. Disapproving. I laughed out loud when he went away with the supper-things. He behaves exactly as if *I* ought to be ashamed.

He won't be caught by the door trick again. There aren't any loose stones. All solidly concreted in. I suppose he thought of that as well as of everything else.

I've spent most of today thinking. About me. What will happen to me? I've never felt the mystery of the future so much as here. What will happen? What will happen?

It's not only now, in this situation. When I get away. What shall I do? I want to marry, I want to have children, I want to prove to myself that all marriages needn't be like D and M's. I know exactly the sort of person I want to marry, someone with a mind like G.P.'s, only much nearer my own age, and with the looks I like. And without his one horrid weakness. But then I want to use my feelings about life. I don't want to use my skill vainly, for its own sake. But I want to *make* beauty. And marriage and being a mother terrifies me for that reason. Getting sucked down into the house and the house things and the baby-world and the child-world and the cooking-world and the shopping-world. I have a feeling a lazy-cow me would welcome it, would forget what I once wanted to do, and I would just become a Great Female Cabbage. Or I would have to do miserable work like illustrating, or even commercial stuff, to keep the home going. Or turn into a bitchy ginny misery like M (no, I couldn't be like her). Or worst of all be like Caroline, running along pathetically after modern art and modern ideas and never catching up with them because she's someone quite different at heart and yet can never see it.

I think and think down here. I understand things I haven't really thought about before.

3

Answer these questions.

1 How did Frederick actually capture Miranda? Do you think he had carefully planned all the details of the capture beforehand?
2 In the last paragraph of the first extract the sentences start with a pronoun, except for one sentence in the second half: 'And then suddenly she went limp.' What effect does this sentence have?
3 Which phrases used by the critics on the back cover of the book are borne out by the first extract?
4 Describe the place where Miranda was imprisoned.
5 Who do you think these people are: D and M; G.P.; Caroline?
6 What effect has Miranda's imprisonment had on her?
7 What impressions do you have of Frederick and Miranda from these two extracts?
8 How do you think the story ends?
9 Has reading the two extracts made you want to read the whole novel? Why?/Why not?

4

Both extracts are written in a colloquial style, as if the two characters were talking to the reader. Try to guess from the text what these colloquial phrases mean:

Extract 1

talking nineteen to the dozen (line 4)
dashed out (line 15)
I flashed a look down the road (line 21/22)
She struggled like the dickens (line 25)
I was ready to bolt for it (line 28)

Extract 2

getting sucked down into the house (line 40/41)
a lazy-cow me (line 43)
a Great Female Cabbage (line 44)
a bitchy ginny misery (line 46/47)

Find the Title

1

Play this game in pairs. You are going to find the titles that belong to ten pictures taken from the front covers of ten novels.

1 Each of you will look at the pictures from the front covers of five novels and the back cover texts of five *different* novels. Your partner has the front cover pictures that belong to your back cover texts. You have the front cover pictures that belong to your partner's back cover texts.

   Student A: look at page 92. Student B: look at page 102.
   DO NOT SHOW YOUR PICTURES TO YOUR PARTNER! Study your pictures and silently read your back cover texts.
2 Student A:
   Describe your five pictures to B. Describe both what you can see in the pictures and the overall impression that each one gives you. B will tell you what he/she thinks the title for each of your pictures is.
3 Student B
   Describe your five pictures to A in the same way. A will tell you what he/she thinks the title for each of your pictures is.

You can check your answers on page 105.

2

Imagine you are going on a long journey. You want to take something to read with you. Choose one title from the ten. Explain to your partner the reasons for your choice.

Back cover texts: Student A

THE SECRET DIARY OF ADRIAN MOLE AGED 13¾

'... the wry, funny journal of a teenager who believes he's an "undiscovered intellectual" and in love.'
SUNDAY EXPRESS

'... a very funny, not-to-be-missed book which will surely become a classic.'
GOOD HOUSEKEEPING

'At last: a wit to touch the hearts of three generations .... The author's accuracy and comic timing left me wincing with pleasure.'
NEW STATESMAN

'... a marvellous new novel .... it seems set fair to become as much a cult book as *The Catcher in the Rye* .... The book is both touching and screamingly funny.'
JILLY COOPER

'I not only wept, I howled and hooted and had to get up and walk round the room and wipe my eyes so that I could go on reading.'
TOM SHARPE

1 *The Secret Diary of Adrian Mole aged 13¾* by Sue Townsend

'It was a bad investment, I knew, this affection, and one that would leave me in the dark and cold in the years to come'

Rosamund had managed to put off the problem of sex until she spends an evening with George. Ironically, that first sexual experience leaves her pregnant, and, having failed to decide not to have it, she finds herself an unmarried mother.

How she faces up to this predicament and all its trials is the subject of this direct, funny and deeply touching novel. It is compulsive reading of the highest order.

Cover illustration by Alan Adler

2 *The Millstone* by Margaret Drabble

Eleven short stories – each a delightful miniature capturing the unique atmosphere of India.

Set in contemporary Bombay and other cities, they reflect the kaleidoscope of urban life – evoking the colour, sounds and white-hot heat of the city. Warm, perceptive, humorous and touched with sadness, Anita Desai's stories are peopled with intensely individual characters – the man spiritually transformed by the surface textures of a melon; the American wife who, homesick for the verdant farmlands of Vermont, turns to the hippies in the Indian hills; the painter living in a slum who fills his canvases with flowers, birds and landscapes he has never seen ...

'Absolutely first-rate' – Hermione Lee in the *Observer*

'Sensitive, delicate and successful ... they convey with gentle authority a sense of what it is like to live in that confusing country' – *Sunday Telegraph*

3 *Games at Twilight* by Anita Desai

Fantastic, frightening, but entirely plausible, John Wyndham's famous story of a world dominated by monstrous, stinging plants catches the imagination like the best of H. G. Wells.

'One of Great Britain's most serious and literate pioneers of intelligent science fiction ... Wyndham always wrote well and imaginatively' – *Financial Times*

Cover illustration by Peter Lord

4 *The Day of the Triffids* by John Wyndham

Barbara Pym's 'unpretentious, subtle, accomplished novels ... are for me the finest examples of high comedy to have appeared in England during the past 75 years'
LORD DAVID CECIL, SUNDAY TIMES

Barbara Pym's sensitive wit and artistry are at their most sparkling in *Quartet in Autumn*. Combining an acute eye for the eccentricities of everyday life with her unique talent for illuminating human frailties, she has created a world which is both extraordinary and totally familiar.

'Spectacular ... powerful'
SUNDAY TIMES

'Very funny and keenly observant of the ridiculous as well as the pathetic in humanity'
FINANCIAL TIMES

5 *Quartet in Autumn* by Barbara Pym

Front cover pictures: Student A

1

2

3

4

5

On the Bookshelf

1 The titles of these books all relate to the names of their authors. Match each title with the most appropriate name. The first one is done for you.

1 Rice Growing	by	☐ Arthur Mometer
2 The Burglar		[1] Paddy Field
3 Home Heating		☐ Henrietta Mann
4 The Cannibal's Daughter		☐ Eileen Dover
5 On the Beach		☐ Percy Vere
6 Keeping Cheerful		☐ C Shaw
7 A Cliff-Top Tragedy		☐ Mona Lott
8 Try Again		☐ Robin Banks

2 Now invent some suitable titles for these authors:

1 Mike Robe
2 I Scream
3 R U Short
4 Eliza Wake
5 Laurie Driver
6 I C Blast
7 Amos Quito

Titles and authors taken from *1000 Jokes for Kids of All Ages* (Ward Lock)

The Arts Council Meeting

Role-play

The Situation

Roseworth is a medium-sized 'new' town 80 miles north-west of London. It has a population of 125,000. Its main industries are car manufacturing, the making of tools, and market gardening.

Two years ago an Arts Council was set up in the town with the aim of 'fostering the arts'. The borough authority very generously allocated 5 per cent of its annual budget to the Arts Council. This money is to be awarded annually to the proposed project which, in the view of the Council, 'will make a significant contribution to the cultural life of our town and surrounding district'.

This year five projects have been proposed:
1 A new theatre, which will present plays in repertory
2 A new cinema, which will show mainly film classics
3 An art centre
4 A fund to help and encourage new writers
5 A youth orchestra

A meeting of the Arts Council has been called to decide which of the five projects should be accepted. It will be attended by the five Arts Council members and by a spokesman for each of the five groups who have proposed a project.

The members of the Arts Council include:

1 the Chairperson
2 the Mayor/Mayoress of Roseworth
3 a local MP
4 the arts critic of *The Voice*, the main daily newspaper of Roseworth
5 Dame Sybil Flushwood, a well-known local patron of the arts

Here is the agenda for the meeting:

AGENDA

1 Welcome to all present from Chairperson
2 Members of Council introduce themselves to Project Spokesmen
3 Project Spokesmen introduce themselves
4 Spokesmen in turn describe project proposals
5 Questions and open discussion
6 Vote to select project
7 Any other business.

Roles

Read only the role that has been assigned to you. If the role does not give you a name, invent one, e.g. Mr/Miss/Mrs Lesley Black.

Members of the Arts Council

Chairperson
You are a member of the local town council. You are interested in the arts and are yourself a writer of short stories. As a member of the town council, you are interested in choosing the project that you feel will be of benefit to as many people as possible in the town.

Mayor/Mayoress of Roseworth
You are very proud of your town and its progress during recent years. You are generally interested in promoting the arts and developing the town's cultural life. You would be in favour of the project which will bring the town the most prestige.

Local MP
Although you are interested in the proposed projects, you are concerned about the economic situation in the whole country and the recent cutbacks in government spending. You therefore feel that to spend money on *any* of the projects is a bit of a luxury.

Newspaper arts critic
You feel that the cultural life of the town is sadly lacking. You are interested in quality rather than quantity and would support the project which will best enhance the intellectual life of the town.

Dame Sybil Flushwood
You live in a large house just outside the town, where your family has lived since the fifteenth century. You made your name as an actress in the theatre, and although you have retired from the theatre, you are well-known in the Roseworth area as a patron of the arts.

Spokesmen for the five projects

Spokesman for the new theatre project
You would like to put across the following points to support your project: At present there is only one theatre in Roseworth. It is not in very good condition and is poorly equipped. Most of the plays presented are poor imitations of London West End 'hits'. A new, well-equipped, modern theatre would present the best in drama: the classics, good new plays, as well as more lightweight entertaining plays. A small permanent company of professional actors and actresses would contribute greatly to the cultural life in the town.

Spokesman for the cinema project
You would like to put across the following points in support of your project: At present there are only two cinemas in Roseworth, both of which show either poor-quality old movies, or popular box-office hits. Also, both cinemas may be described as 'flea-pits'. There is growing demand for quality films to be shown, as evidenced by the very successful local film society which at present uses the Town Hall to show films. Also, since the building of a new university near the town, there are many students in the area.

Spokesman for an art centre
You would like to put across the following points in support of your project: There is nowhere in Roseworth which caters to the fine arts: no art gallery, only a room at the public library which occasionally has a very limited display of paintings by local artists. An art centre would fill this gap, as well as provide facilities, especially for young people, to attend art classes. A questionnaire circulated in the town earlier this year met with a very positive response: there is great interest in this project among local residents.

Spokesman for a fund to encourage new writers
You would like to put across the following points in support of your project: Many young writers do not have the opportunity to devote themselves to writing because of their need to earn a living. If such a fund were established, competitions could be held in various categories: poetry, drama, fiction, non-fiction, etc. Prizewinners would be awarded sufficient sums of money annually to allow them to work on their writings. A local county literary magazine proves that there is great potential literary talent in the area.

Spokesman for a youth orchestra
You would like to put across the following points in support of the project: There is at present a small group of young amateur musicians who meet and practise in the local church hall. Last year they won first prize in a competition for amateur music groups held at York, in the north of England. If this group were given professional status, they would be able to develop their potential further as well as enhance the town's prestige.

Devised by Anthony Fagin, Regent School of English

A Short Story Writer: Frank O'Connor

Frank O'Connor (1903–1966) is a pseudonym of Michael O'Donovan, a largely self-educated Irish writer who, after service in the Irish Republican Army (against the British), became a librarian, a director of the celebrated Abbey Theatre (Dublin), and a member of the Irish Academy of Letters. O'Connor is remembered primarily for approximately twenty-five volumes of short stories. Although he felt his gifts were primarily lyrical, he was a rewriter of great tenacity, and some of his stories went through fifty revisions.

On the cassette you can listen to *Christmas Morning*. Try to listen *without* reading the text.

Sit back comfortably, relax, and enjoy listening!

Christmas Morning

I never really liked my brother, Sonny. From the time he was a baby he was always the mother's pet and always chasing her to tell her what mischief I was up to. Mind you, I was usually up to something. Until I was nine or ten I was never much good at school, and I really believe it was to spite me that he was so smart at his books. He seemed to know by instinct that this was what Mother had set her heart on, and you might almost say he spelt himself into her favour.

'Mummy,' he'd say, 'will I call Larry in to his t-e-a?' or: 'Mummy, the k-e-t-e-l is boiling,' and, of course, when he was wrong she'd correct him, and next time he'd have it right and there would be no standing him. 'Mummy,' he'd say, 'aren't I a good speller?' Cripes, we could all be good spellers if we went on like that!

Mind you, it wasn't that I was stupid. Far from it. I was just restless and not able to fix my mind for long on any one thing. I'd do the lessons for the year before, or the lessons for the year after: what I couldn't stand were the lessons we were supposed to be doing at the time. In the evenings I used to go out and play with the Doherty gang. Not, again, that I was rough, but I liked the excitement, and for the life of me I couldn't see what attracted Mother about education.

'Can't you do your lessons first and play after?' she'd say, getting white with indignation. 'You ought to be ashamed of yourself that your baby brother can read better than you.'

She didn't seem to understand that I wasn't, because there didn't seem to me to be anything particularly praiseworthy about reading, and it struck me as an occupation better suited to a sissy kid like Sonny.

'The dear knows what will become of you,' she'd say. 'If only you'd stick to your books you might be something good like a clerk or an engineer.'

'I'll be a clerk, Mummy,' Sonny would say smugly.

'Who wants to be an old clerk?' I'd say, just to annoy him. 'I'm going to be a soldier.'

'The dear knows, I'm afraid that's all you'll ever be fit for,' she would add with a sigh.

I couldn't help feeling at times that she wasn't all there. As if there was anything better a fellow could be!

Coming on to Christmas, with the days getting shorter and the shopping crowds bigger, I began to think of all the things I might get from Santa Claus. The Dohertys said there was no Santa Claus, only what your father and mother gave you, but the Dohertys were a rough class of children you wouldn't expect Santa to come to anyway. I was rooting round for whatever information I could pick up about him, but there didn't seem to be much. I was no hand with a pen, but if a letter would do any good I was ready to chance writing to him. I had plenty of initiative and was always writing off for free samples and prospectuses.

'Ah, I don't know will he come at all this year,' Mother said with a worried air. 'He has enough to do looking after steady boys who mind their lessons without bothering about the rest.'

'He only comes to good spellers, Mummy,' said Sonny. 'Isn't that right?'

'He comes to any little boy who does his best, whether he's a good speller or not,' Mother said firmly.

Well, I did my best. God knows I did! It wasn't my fault if, four days before the holidays, Flogger Dawley gave us sums we couldn't do, and Peter Doherty and myself had to go on the lang. It wasn't for love of it, for take it from me, December is no month for mitching, and we spent most of our time sheltering from the rain in a store on the quays. The only mistake we made was imagining we could keep it up till the holidays without being spotted. That showed real lack of foresight.

Of course, Flogger Dawley noticed and sent home word to know what was keeping me. When I came in on the third day the mother gave me a look I'll never forget, and said: 'Your dinner is there.' She was too full to talk. When I tried to explain to her about Flogger Dawley and the sums she brushed it aside and said: 'You have no word.' I saw then it wasn't the langing she minded but the lies, though I still didn't see how you could lang without lying. She didn't speak to me for days. And even then I couldn't make out what she saw in education, or why she wouldn't let me grow up naturally like anyone else.

To make things worse, it stuffed Sonny up more than ever. He had the air of one saying: 'I don't know what they'd do without me in this blooming house.' He stood at the front door, leaning against the jamb with his hands in his trouser pockets, trying to make himself look like Father, and shouted to the other kids so that he could be heard all over the road.

'Larry isn't left go out. He went on the lang with Peter Doherty and me mother isn't talking to him.'

And at night, when we were in bed, he kept it up.

'Santa Claus won't bring you anything this year, aha!'

'Of course he will,' I said.

'How do you know?'

'Why wouldn't he?'

'Because you went on the lang with Doherty. I wouldn't play with them Doherty fellows.'

'You wouldn't be left.'

'I wouldn't play with them. They're no class. They had the bobbies up to the house.'

'And how would Santa know I was on the lang with Peter Doherty?' I growled, losing patience with the little prig.

'Of course he'd know. Mummy would tell him.'

'And how could Mummy tell him and he up at the North Pole? Poor Ireland, she's rearing them yet! 'Tis easy seen you're only an old baby.'

'I'm not a baby, and I can spell better than you, and Santa won't bring you anything.'

'We'll see whether he will or not,' I said sarcastically, doing the old man on him.

But, to tell the God's truth, the old man was only bluff. You could never tell what powers these superhuman chaps would have of knowing what you were up to. And I had a bad conscience about the langing because I'd never before seen the mother like that.

That was the night I decided that the only sensible thing to do was to see Santa myself and explain to him. Being a man, he'd probably understand. In those days I was a good-looking kid and had a way with me when I liked. I had only to smile nicely at one old gent on the North Mall to get a penny from him, and I felt if only I could get Santa by himself I could do the same with him and maybe get something worth while from him. I wanted a model railway: I was sick of Ludo and Snakes-and-Ladders.

I started to practise lying awake, counting five hundred and then a thousand, and trying to hear first eleven, then midnight, from Shandon. I felt sure Santa would be round by midnight, seeing that he'd be coming from the north, and would have the whole of the South Side to do afterwards. In some ways I was very farsighted. The only trouble was the things I was farsighted about.

I was so wrapped up in my own calculations that I had little attention to spare for Mother's difficulties. Sonny and I used to go to town with her, and while she was shopping we stood outside a toyshop in the North Main Street, arguing about what we'd like for Christmas.

On Christmas Eve when Father came home from work and gave her the housekeeping money, she stood looking at it doubtfully while her face grew white.

'Well?' he snapped, getting angry. 'What's wrong with that?'

'What's wrong with it?' she muttered. 'On Christmas Eve!'

'Well,' he asked truculently, sticking his hands in his trouser pockets as though to guard what was left, 'do you think I get more because it's Christmas?'

'Lord God,' she muttered distractedly. 'And not a bit of cake in the house, nor a candle, nor anything.'

'All right,' he shouted, beginning to stamp. 'How much will the candle be?'

'Ah, for pity's sake,' she cried, 'will you give me the money and not argue like that before the children? Do you think I'll leave them with nothing on the one day of the year?'

'Bad luck to you and your children!' he snarled. 'Am I to be slaving from one year's end to another for you to be throwing it away on toys? Here,' he added, tossing two half-crowns on the table, 'that's all you're going to get, so make the most of it.'

'I suppose the publicans will get the rest,' she said bitterly.

Later she went into town, but did not bring us with her, and returned with a lot of parcels, including the Christmas candle. We waited for Father to come home to his tea, but he didn't so we had our own tea and a slice of Christmas cake each, and then Mother put Sonny on a chair with the holy-water stoup to sprinkle the candle, and when he lit it she said: 'The light of heaven to our souls.' I could see she was upset because Father wasn't in—it should be the oldest and youngest. When we hung up our stockings at bedtime he was still out.

Then began the hardest couple of hours I ever put in. I was mad with sleep but afraid of losing the model railway, so I lay for a while, making up things to say to Santa when he came. They varied in tone from frivolous to grave, for some old gents like kids to be modest and well-spoken, while others prefer them with spirit. When I had rehearsed them all I tried to wake Sonny to keep me company, but that kid slept like the dead.

Eleven struck from Shandon, and soon after I heard the latch, but it was only Father coming home.

'Hello, little girl,' he said, letting on to be surprised at finding Mother waiting up for him, and then broke into a self-conscious giggle. 'What have you up so late?'

'Do you want your supper?' she asked shortly.

'Ah, no, no,' he replied. 'I had a bit of pig's cheek at Daneen's on my way up (Daneen was my uncle). I'm very fond of a bit of pig's cheek. . . . My goodness, is it that late?' he exclaimed, letting on to be astonished. 'If I knew that I'd have gone to the North Chapel for midnight Mass. I'd like to hear the *Adeste* again. That's a hymn I'm very fond of—a most touching hymn:'

Then he began to hum it falsetto.

Adeste fideles
Solus domus dagus.

Father was very fond of Latin hymns, particularly when he had a drop in, but as he had no notion of the words he made them up as he went along, and this always drove Mother mad.

'Ah, you disgust me!' she said in a scalded voice, and closed the room door behind her. Father laughed as he thought it a great joke; and he struck a match to light his pipe and for a while puffed at it noisily. The light under the door dimmed and went out but he continued to sing emotionally.

Dixie medearo
Tutum tonum tantum
Venite adoremus.

He had it all wrong but the effect was the same on me. To save my life I couldn't keep awake.

Coming on to dawn, I woke with the feeling that something dreadful had happened. The whole house was quiet, and the little bedroom that looked out on the foot and a half of back yard was pitch-dark. It was only when I glanced at the window that I saw how all the silver had drained out of the sky. I jumped out of bed to feel my stocking, well knowing that the worst had happened. Santa had come while I was asleep, and gone away with an entirely false impression of me, because all he had left me was some sort of book, folded up, a pen and pencil, and a tuppenny bag of sweets. Not even Snakes-and-Ladders! For a while I was too stunned even to think. A fellow who was able to drive over rooftops and climb down chimneys without getting stuck—God, wouldn't you think he'd know better?

Then I began to wonder what that foxy boy, Sonny, had. I went to his side of the bed and felt his stocking. For all his spelling and sucking-up he hadn't done so much better, because, apart from a bag of sweets like mine, all Santa had left him was a popgun, one that fired a cork on a piece of string and which you could get in any huckster's shop for sixpence.

All the same, the fact remained that it was a gun, and a gun was better than a book any day of the week. The Dohertys had a gang, and the gang fought the Strawberry Lane kids who tried to play football on our road. That gun would be very useful to me in many ways, while it would be lost on Sonny who wouldn't be let play with the gang, even if he wanted to.

Then I got the inspiration, as it seemed to me, direct from heaven. Suppose I took the gun and gave Sonny the book! Sonny would never be any good in the gang: he was fond of spelling and a studious child like him could learn a lot of spellings from a book like mine. As he hadn't seen Santa any more than I had, what he hadn't seen wouldn't grieve him. I was doing no harm to anyone; in fact, if Sonny only knew, I was doing him a good turn which he might have cause to thank me for later. That was one thing I was always keen on, doing good turns. Perhaps this was Santa's intention the whole time and he had merely become confused between us. It was a mistake that might happen to anyone. So I put the book, the pencil, and the pen into Sonny's stocking and the popgun into my own, and returned to bed and slept again. As I say, in those days I had plenty of initiative.

It was Sonny who woke me, shaking me to tell me that Santa had come and left me a gun. I let on to be surprised and rather disappointed in the gun, and to divert his mind from it made him show me his picture book, and cracked it up to the skies.

As I knew, that kid was prepared to believe anything, and nothing would do him then but to take the presents in to show Father and Mother. This was a bad moment for me. After the way she had behaved about the langing, I distrusted Mother, though I had the consolation of believing that the only person who could contradict me was now somewhere up by the North Pole. That gave me a certain confidence, so Sonny and I burst in with our presents shouting: 'Look what Santa Claus brought!'

Father and Mother woke, and Mother smiled, but only for an instant. As she looked at me her face changed. I knew that look; I knew it only too well. It was the same she had worn the day I came home from langing, when she said I had no word.

'Larry,' she said in a low voice, 'where did you get that gun?'

'Santa left it in my stocking, Mummy,' I said, trying to put on an injured air, though it baffled me how she guessed that he hadn't. 'He did, honest.'

'You stole it from that poor child's stocking while he was asleep,' she said, her voice quivering with indignation. 'Larry, Larry, how could you be so mean?'

'Now, now, now,' Father said deprecatingly, 'tis Christmas morning.'

'Ah,' she said with real passion, 'it's easy it comes to you. Do you think I want my son to grow up a liar and a thief?'

'Ah, what thief, woman?' he said testily. 'Have sense, can't you?' He was as cross if you interrupted him in his benevolent moods as if they were of the other sort, and this one was probably exacerbated by a feeling of guilt for his behaviour of the night before. 'Here, Larry,' he said, reaching out for the money on the bedside table, 'here's sixpence for you and one for Sonny. Mind you don't lose it now!'

But I looked at Mother and saw what was in her eyes. I burst out crying, threw the popgun on the floor, and ran bawling out of the house before anyone on the road was awake. I rushed up the lane behind the house and threw myself on the wet grass.

I understood it all, and it was almost more than I could bear; that there was no Santa Claus, as the Dohertys said, only Mother trying to scrape together a few coppers from the housekeeping; that Father was mean and common and a drunkard, and that she had been relying on me to raise her out of the misery of the life she was leading. And I knew that the look in her eyes was the fear that, like my father, I should turn out to be mean and common and a drunkard.

Describe and draw

Pictures for Player B

Back cover texts: Student B

Henry Pulling, a retired bank manager, meets his septuagenarian Aunt Augusta for the first time in over fifty years at what he supposes to be his mother's funeral.

Soon after, she persuades Henry to abandon Southwood, his dahlias and the Major next door to travel *her* way, Brighton, Paris, Istanbul, Paraguay...through Aunt Augusta, a veteran of Europe's hotel bedrooms, Henry joins a shiftless, twilight society; mixing with hippies, war criminals, CIA men; smoking pot, breaking all the currency regulations...coming alive after a dull suburban lifetime.

In *Travels With My Aunt* Graham Greene not only gives us intoxicating entertainment but also confronts us with some of the deepest and most perplexing of human dilemmas.

1 *Travels with my Aunt*
by Graham Greene

"An authentic work of art"*

Toby Hood, a young Englishman, shuns the politics and the causes his liberal parents passionately support. Living in Johannesburg as a representative of his family's publishing company, Toby moves easily, carelessly, between the complacent wealthy white suburbs and the seething, vibrantly alive black townships. His friends include a wide variety of people, from mining directors to black journalists and musicians, and Toby's colonial-style weekends are often interspersed with clandestine evenings spent in black shanty towns.

Toby's friendship with Steven Sithole, a dashing, embittered young African, touches him in ways he never thought possible, and when Steven's own sense of independence from the rules of society leads to tragedy, Toby's life is changed forever.

"[Gordimer's] characters are universal. It is to the moments of greatest stress, when frail structures of idealism are being tested by shaking realities, that Miss Gordimer gives the form of literature."
—**The New York Times*

"A triumphant success"—*The Observer*

2 *A World of Strangers*
by Nadine Gordimer

For a shy sixteen-year-old girl, Christmas with the Lancing family was to be her first, exhilarating taste of growing-up.

There's delightful Lucy, Gerald (very good at ice skating), Elspeth (interested in natural history, especially caterpillars), Deborah (with her hair up, almost overwhelmingly sophisticated); and then there's Rupert, recently down from Cambridge, living a bohemian existence in London and so terrifyingly handsome that, well...he must be teasing her?

All the longing, excitement and poignant comedy of adolescence is captured in Elizabeth Jane Howard's beautifully observed story of a young girl growing up in the years around the First World War.

'Interesting and original...she has true imagination and a kind of sensuous power...she can also draw scenes with ironic brilliance...hers seems to me to be a remarkable talent' – Antonia White in the *New Statesman*

Winner of the John Llewelyn Rhys Memorial Prize

3 *The Beautiful Visit*
by Elizabeth Jane Howard

What, you've never read
a Roald Dahl novel?

I have decided to permit the public yet another glimpse into my Uncle Oswald's life. (Uncle Oswald is, if you remember, the greatest rogue, bounder, connoisseur, bon vivant and fornicator of all time.) The section chosen comes from Volume XX and many famous names are mentioned and there is obviously a grave risk that families and friends are going to take offence...

Uncle Oswald discovers the electrifying properties of the Sudanese Blister Beetle and the gorgeous Yasmin Howcomely, a girl absolutely soaked in sex, and sets about seducing all the great men of the time for his own wicked, irreverent reasons.

'Very saucy' – *Daily Express*

'Deliciously silly' – *Observer*

'Dahl could not be boring if he tried... raunchy exuberance and cheeky entertainment' – *Sunday Express*

'I long for a sequel' – *Now!*

'Immense fun' – *Daily Telegraph*

4 *My Uncle Oswald* by Roald Dahl

Cider With Rosie puts on record
the England that was traded
for the petrol engine.
Recalling life in a remote Cotswold
village some fifty years ago,
Laurie Lee conveys
the semi-peasant spirit of
a thousand-years-old tradition.

'This poet, whose prose is quick
and bright as a snake...
a gay, impatient,
jaunty and in parts slightly
mocking book;
a prose poem that flashes and
winks like a prism' –
H. E. Bates in the (London) *Sunday Times*

First published in the United States
under the title *Edge of Day: Boyhood in the West of England*

5 *Cider with Rosie*
by Laurie Lee

Front cover pictures: Student B

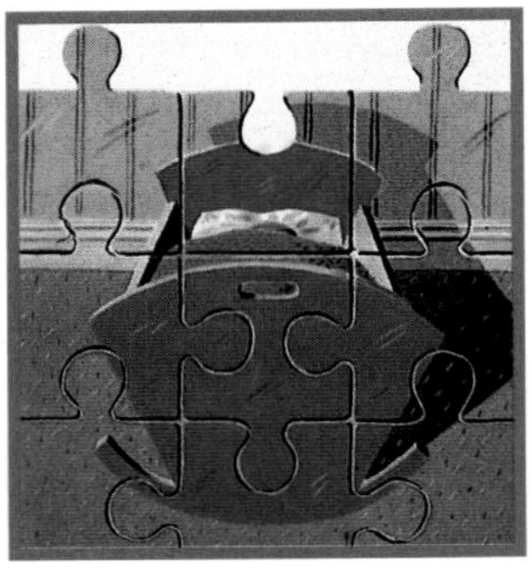

1

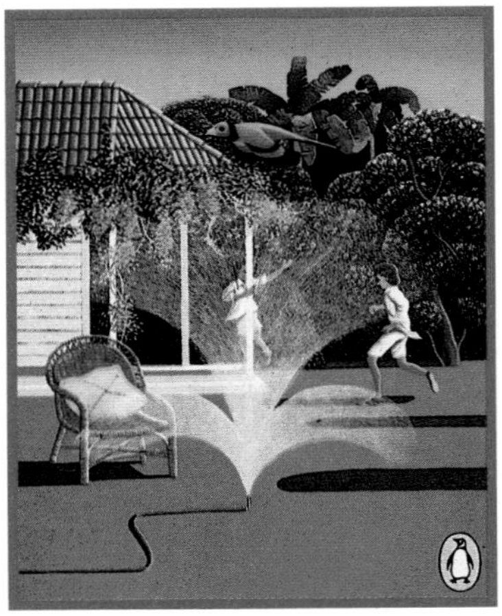

2

3

4

5

Solutions

Attitudes to Education

Attitudes to Education

1 Which one of the following groups do you think should have the greatest influence in deciding what is taught in each school?

The Government	**9%**
Local authorities	**12%**
Parent groups	**29%**
Teachers	**44%**
Don't know	**6%**

2 Do you think girls are better off going to single-sex or mixed schools?

Single-sex schools	**21%**
Mixed schools	**73%**
Don't know	**6%**

3 Do you think boys are better off going to single-sex or mixed schools?

Single-sex schools	**20%**
Mixed schools	**73%**
Don't know	**7%**

4 How strongly do you agree or disagree that 'It is not as important for girls to go to college or university as for boys'?

	All	**Men**	**Women**
Strongly agree	**4%**	**4%**	**4%**
Agree fairly strongly	**13%**	**14%**	**12%**
Disagree fairly strongly	**36%**	**41%**	**31%**
Disagree strongly	**46%**	**40%**	**51%**
Don't know	**1%**	**1%**	**2%**

5 **(a)** Which three of these subjects are the most important at school nowadays?
(b) Which three of these subjects are the least important?

Most Important		**Least Important**
81%	mathematics	**0.5%**
79%	mother tongue	**1%**
29%	computer studies	**4%**
22%	science	**4%**
15%	foreign languages	**17%**
10%	business studies	**10%**
8%	technical subjects	**37%**
8%	religious education	**37%**
7%	sex education	**28%**
6%	home economics	**16%**
6%	social studies	**19%**
6%	economics	**6%**
6%	history	**14%**
6%	physical education	**18%**
3%	geography	**8%**
3%	woodwork/metalwork	**49%**
2%	peace studies	**49%**
1%	art	**35%**

Brain Teasers

1 £87.50
We can find the answer by working backwards. In the third bank Mr Smith must have been loaned half of what he deposited: £50. He must have come into the bank with £50. In the second bank Mr Smith must have had £150 before he made the deposit. He must have come into the bank with half that amount: £75. In the first bank Mr Smith must have had £175 before he made his deposit. He must have come into the bank with half that amount: £87.50

2 Mr Taylor is the accountant, Mr Howard is the public relations officer and Mr Miller is the marketing manager.
We can work out this puzzle by a process of elimination. 'The accountant and Mr Miller usually have lunch together' tells us that Mr Miller is not the accountant. Either Mr Taylor or Mr Howard is the accountant. But Mr Taylor has the middle office, so only he could knock on Mr Miller's wall. Mr Taylor must be the accountant. This leaves two jobs: marketing manager and public relations officer. If the marketing manager takes Mr Howard's telephone calls, Mr Howard is not the marketing manager. Nor is he the accountant. He must be the public relations officer. This means that Mr Miller is the marketing manager.

Set for Survival

Here is the second half of the text on page 67.

THE OFFICE

Forget the sandwiches – this is what the well-prepared business person's briefcase should contain:
Casio HL 809 calculator from Boots for totting up your expenses; erasable ball point pen for the crossword; a book, 'Bureaucrats, How to Annoy Them' by R.T. Fishall (Arrow, £1.25), to help you get your own back on the Inland Revenue; the Filofax, an ingenious leather ring binder to which you can add sections for addresses, notes, personal accounts, credit cards (from a large selection, from £6.35 to £44.10, at Chisholms, Kingsway WC2); penknife with bottle opener and corkscrew (£1.60 from Selfridges) for the deskbound lunch; hip flask (£7.99 from Selfridges) for times of crisis; large white handkerchief; safety pins, for presenting a neat front to the world when everything is secretly collapsing; glucose tablets, to give you energy to tackle the rush hour; breath freshener and indigestion tablets, necessary after an expense account lunch with copious alcohol and garlic.
To contain it all: metal briefcase from Inside Out Shop, Covent Garden, WC2 (£27.50).

From *The Observer*

Find the Title

Here are the full covers of the ten books featured in Unit 10.

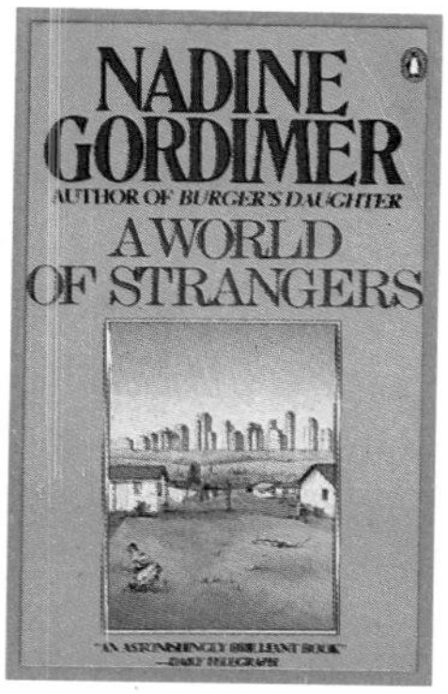

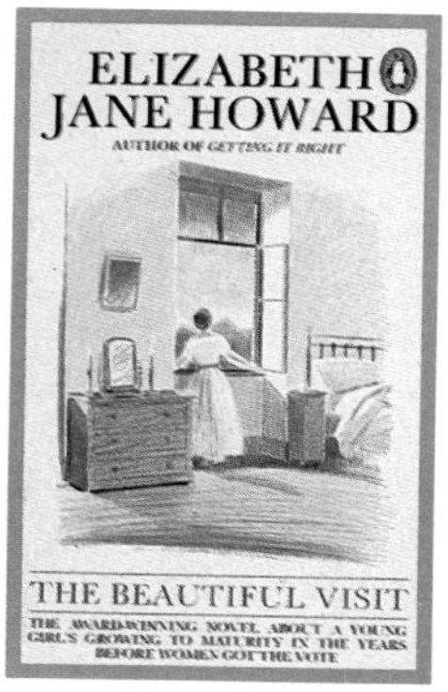

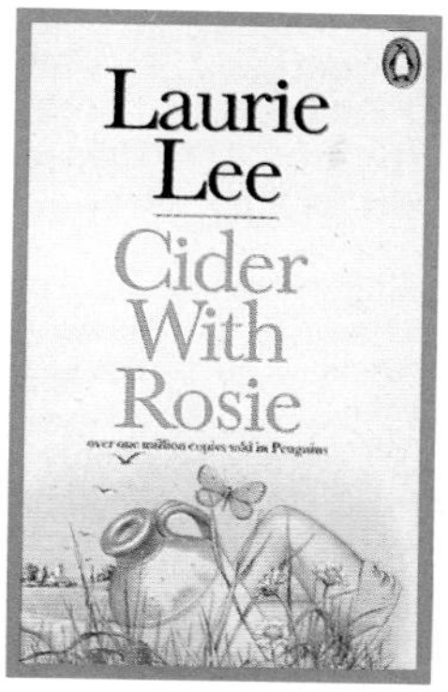

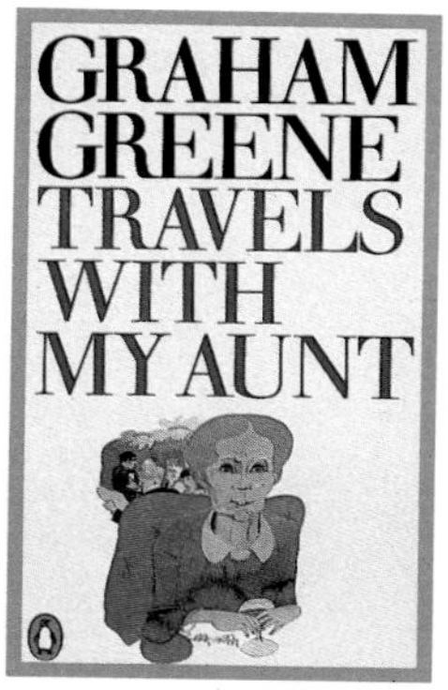

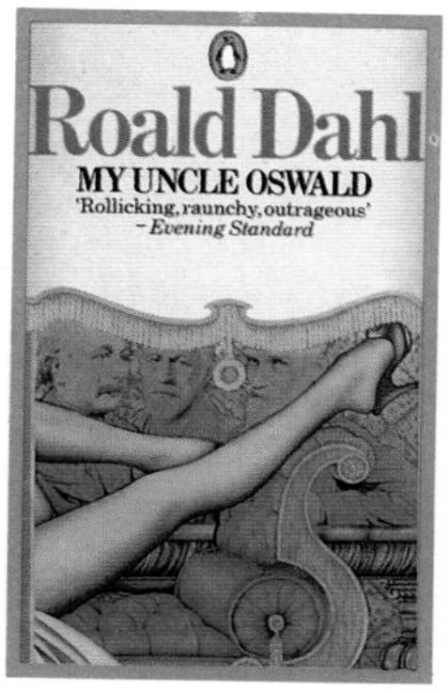

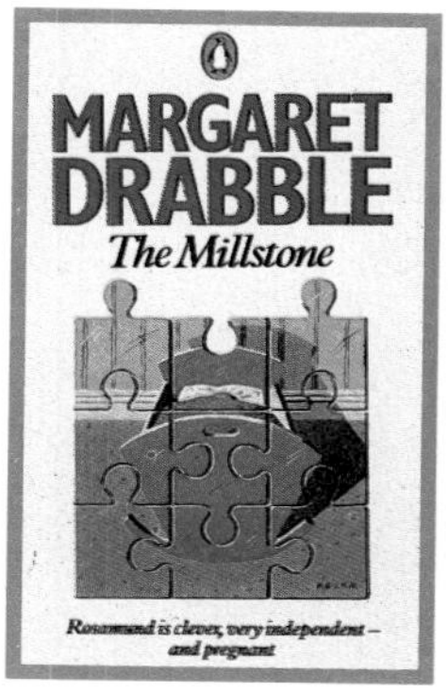

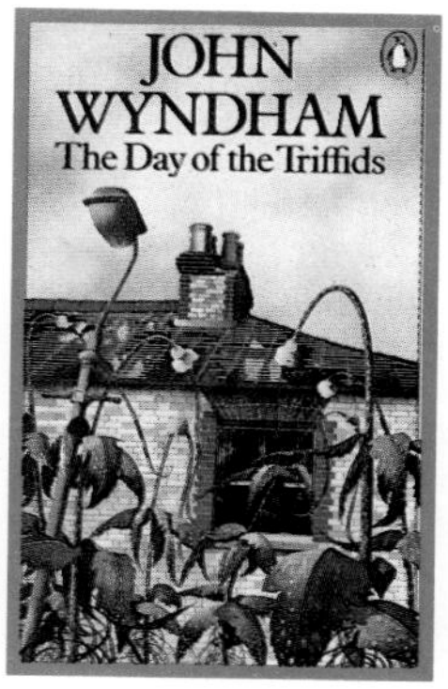

Acknowledgements

The author and publishers would like to thank all the copyright holders for their permission to reproduce the extracts in this book. The sources of the extracts, as well as the authors and publishers, are acknowledged in the text. Further acknowledgements are as follows:

A writer named Wright (p. 4), *Medical Jokes* (p. 20) and *On the Bookshelf* are from *1000 Jokes for Kids of All Ages* © Ward Lock 1979. *Celery Raw* by Ogden Nash (p. 10) is reprinted by permission of Curtis Brown Ltd. The texts and recordings of *English Vines and Wines* (pp. 11–12), *Young Enterprise* (pp. 62–6) and *Drive an Ad!* (pp. 72–3) first appeared in *Business Express* (Modern English Publications). *Kenya Safari*, *Questionnaire* and *Kenya: The Going Rates* (Unit 3) by permission of Kuoni Travel Ltd. *A Warrior Stood Watching* (p. 25) by permission of Tom Tickell. The extract from *Drawing on the Right Side of the Brain* (p. 31) by permission of Souvenir Press Ltd. The extract from *Make the Most of Your Mind* (p.40) by permission of Colt Books Ltd. The recording for *The Ideal Teacher* (p. 50) first appeared in *Playback 2* (Mary Glasgow Publications Ltd.). The two extracts (pp. 51–4) from *The School That I'd Like* © Penguin Books and the contributors 1969 are reprinted by permission of Penguin Books Ltd. *Difficult Tasks for Managers* (pp. 58–61) is reprinted with special permission from *International Management* © McGraw-Hill Publications Company, all rights reserved. The extract (pp. 80–81) from *Who Cares about English Usage?* © David Crystal 1984 is reprinted by permission of Penguin Books Ltd. *The Gift Game* (pp. 86–7) is adapted from Byrne and Rixon ELT Guide 1 'Communication Games' © 1979 The British Council, published by NFER-NELSON Publishing Company Ltd. The extracts (pp. 89–90) from *The Collector* © John Fowles 1963 are reprinted by permission of the author, Jonathan Cape Ltd. and Anthony Sheil Associates Ltd. *Christmas Morning* by Frank O'Connor (pp. 96–100) is reprinted by permission of A. D. Peter & Co. Ltd.

The publishers have been unable to trace the copyright holders of Trials of a Tourist *(p. 30) and of* Freedom in a Pie *(pp. 74–6) and would be pleased to hear from them. They would also be pleased to hear from any other parties who feel they hold rights to any of the texts included.*

The publishers would also like to thank the following for their permission to reproduce photographs, maps, and wine labels:

Heather Angel/Biofotos; Mike Abrahams/Network; Barnaby's Picture Library; The Anthony Blake Photo Library; British Tourist Authority; Gerry Cranham; Jonathan Elford; Gill Fargher; Frithsden; Fotobank; Peter Howe; Lamberhurst Priory; The Observer; Ordnance Survey; Clay Perry; Picturepoint Ltd.; Doug Poole; The Sunday Times; Homer Sykes; Wootton; Jerry Young; Young Enterprises;

and Micro Instruments (Oxford) Ltd. *for their time and assistance.*

Design by:

Shireen Nathoo; Nicky Stratford; Sally Foord-Kelcey.

Illustrations by:

Judy Brown; Penny Dann; Antonia Enthoven; Frank Kennard; David Loftus; Joanna Quinn; Tessa Richardson-Jones; David Simonds.

Commissioned photographs by:

Chris Honeywell; Rob Judges; Mark Mason; Brian Peart/Copies.